HAIKU
Seasons of
Japanese Poetry

俳
句

HAIKU
Seasons of
Japanese Poetry

Edited by
Johanna Brownell

CASTLE BOOKS

For My Mother, Sondra Brownell
With love always

Cover painting by Stephen Addiss

This edition published by
CASTLE BOOKS
a division of Book Sales, Inc.
114 Northfield Avenue
Edison, NJ 08837

Designed by Tony Meisel
Printed in the United States of America

ISBN 0-7858-1372-1

Contents

Introduction

The art of Haiku, one of the most striking and beautiful of poetic forms, was officially born in Japan at the beginning of the Tokugawa shogunate (1603-1770). Originally known as haikai or hokku, this poetic form has always consisted of a three-lined verse of seventeen syllables, arranged in alternating lines of five, seven and five syllables each. The haiku style grew out of the popular pastime known as Renga, in which one or more poets supplied alternating sections to short, five-lined verse then known as *tanka* verse. But unlike the Renga, which was considered more of a game than a true poetic genre, the miniature haikai literary form eventually took on a life of its own. It was first elevated into a high literary form by the seventeenth century poet Matsuo Basho (1644-94), who drew his inspiration from the teaching of ancient religious philosophers, while later artists, including poet Kobayashi Issa (1763-1828) and famed literary critic Masaoka Shiki (1867-1902), revived and enriched its style. Today haiku remains the most popular form of literary expression in Japan while its popularity in the West continues to grow.

Thousands of haiku are composed every year, and for the most part, represent landscapes, seasons, birds, insects, flowers, phases of the moon and other natural phenomena.The Japanese are riveted by the purity and beauty of nature, and have historically conveyed this in their verse through a subtle sense of emotionalism that avoids abstract reasoning and human valorization. While much is lost in translation, the Western reader can still feel the quietude of a summer day, the chill of a winter snow or a sense of awe in the reflection of a landscape that includes the frost-covered tip of Mount

Fuji. Although bound by its concise format, haiku offers a skillful lyricist the ability to create or suggest a scene, a landscape, or a mood that is open to endless interpretation and meaning. It is left to the reader to fill in and interpret the details of a painting suggested by the haiku master.

The Odes that are included here are familiar to almost every Japanese household. They include ancient pearls of Japanese wisdom and personal expressions of life and love that juxtapose the more austere haiku. Each ode contains approximately thirty characters. They do not adhere to a rhyme scheme and, according to tradition, should be read in a somewhat monotonous falsetto voice. Although the odes are not as formally recognized as the haiku, they offer another inspiring expression of Japanese literary culture.

HAIKU

俳

句

A book of verse for thee,
Blown by the autumn breezes o'er
Ten thousand miles of sea.
                    KEI-ON

WINTER

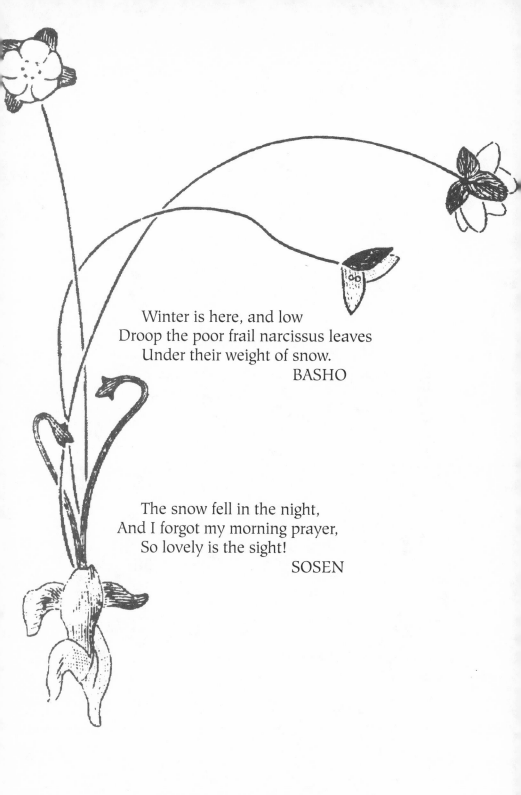

Winter is here, and low
Droop the poor frail narcissus leaves
Under their weight of snow.
                    BASHO

The snow fell in the night,
And I forgot my morning prayer,
So lovely is the sight!
                    SOSEN

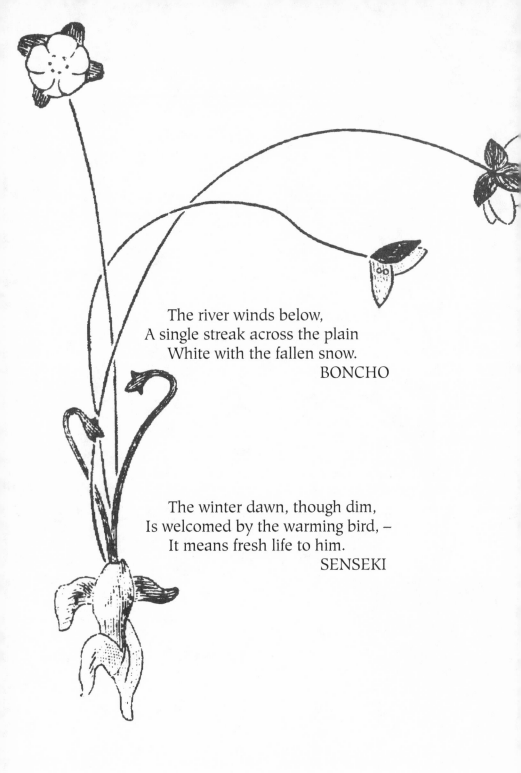

The river winds below,
A single streak across the plain
White with the fallen snow.
BONCHO

The winter dawn, though dim,
Is welcomed by the warming bird, –
It means fresh life to him.
SENSEKI

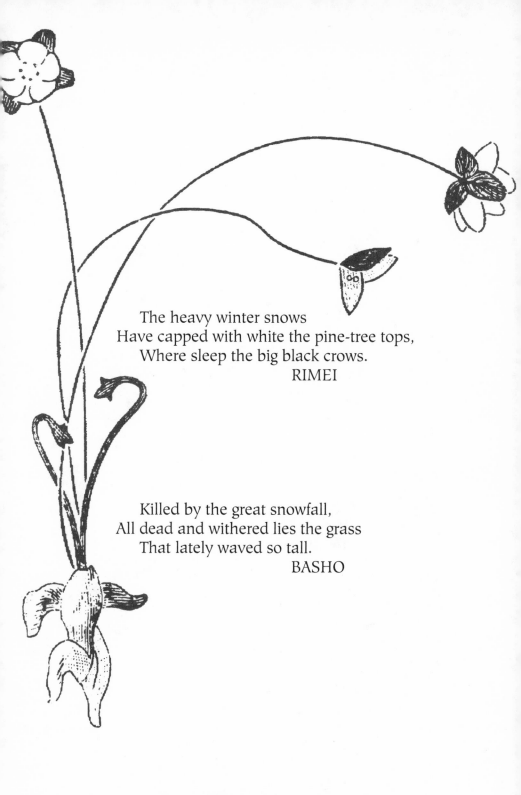

The heavy winter snows
Have capped with white the pine-tree tops,
Where sleep the big black crows.
RIMEI

Killed by the great snowfall,
All dead and withered lies the grass
That lately waved so tall.
BASHO

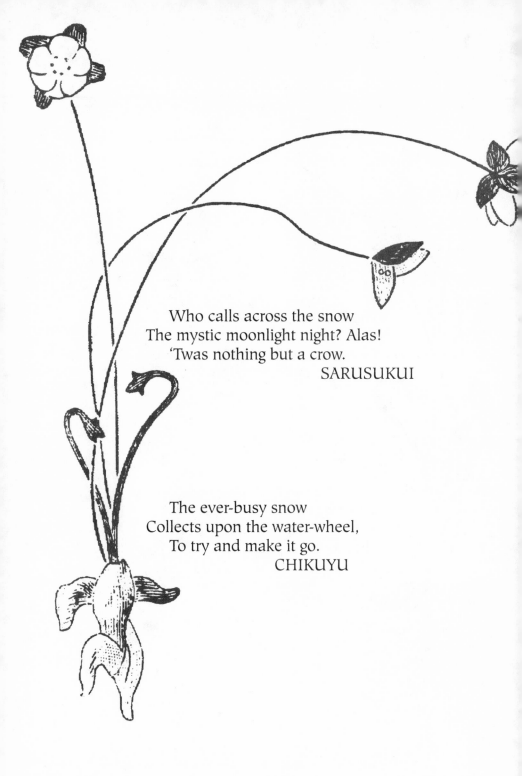

Who calls across the snow
The mystic moonlight night? Alas!
'Twas nothing but a crow.
SARUSUKUI

The ever-busy snow
Collects upon the water-wheel,
To try and make it go.
CHIKUYU

The snow fell in the night,
And people rouse each other up
To see the lovely sight.
RANSETSU

Come out! Come out with me!
'Tis worth a tumble in the snow
The wondrous sight to see.
BASHO

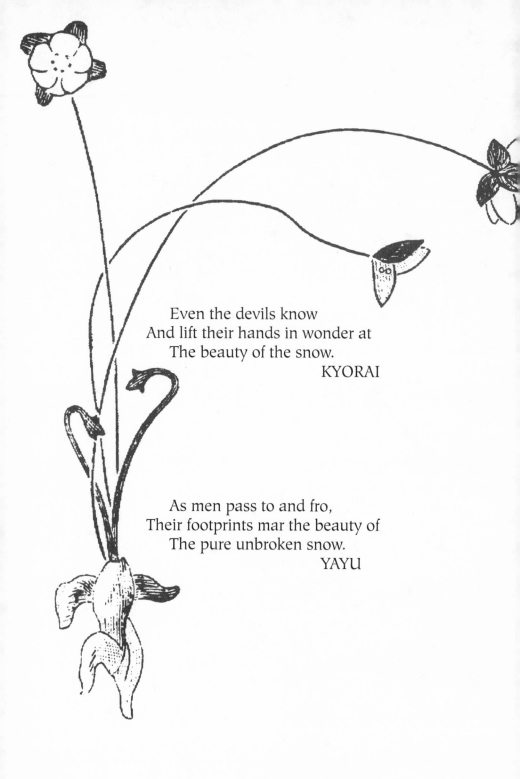

Even the devils know
And lift their hands in wonder at
The beauty of the snow.
                    KYORAI

As men pass to and fro,
Their footprints mar the beauty of
The pure unbroken snow.
                    YAYU

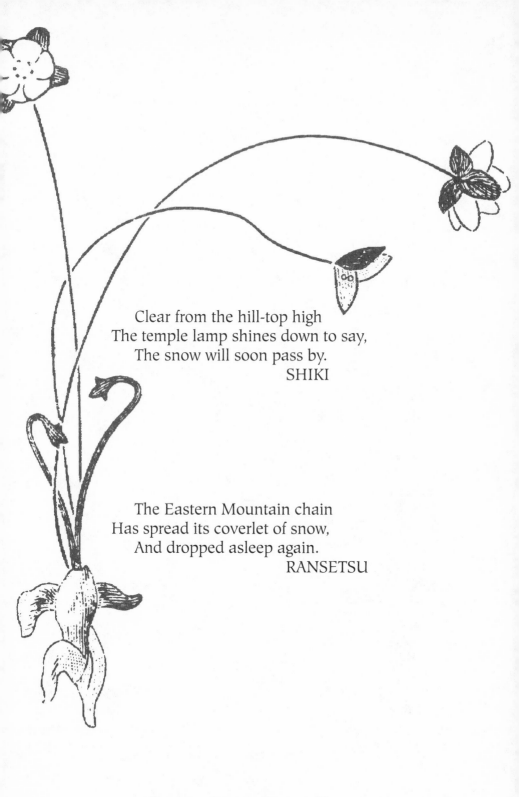

Clear from the hill-top high
The temple lamp shines down to say,
The snow will soon pass by.
SHIKI

The Eastern Mountain chain
Has spread its coverlet of snow,
And dropped asleep again.
RANSETSU

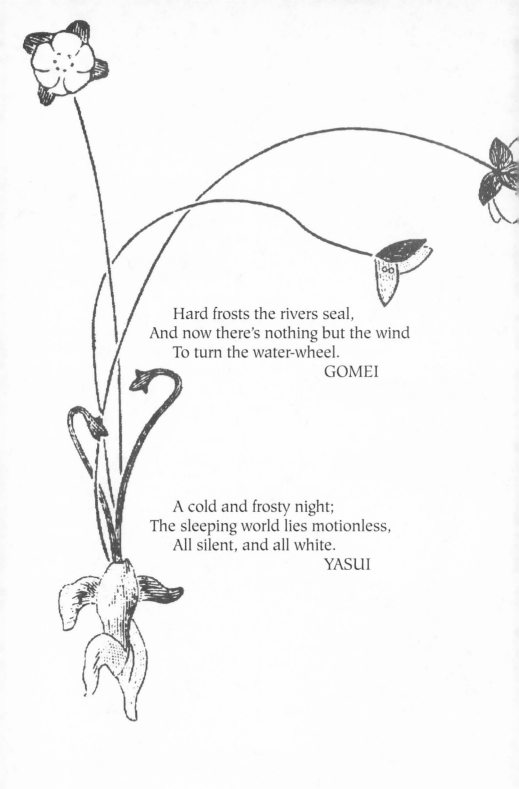

Hard frosts the rivers seal,
And now there's nothing but the wind
To turn the water-wheel.
GOMEI

A cold and frosty night;
The sleeping world lies motionless,
All silent, and all white.
YASUI

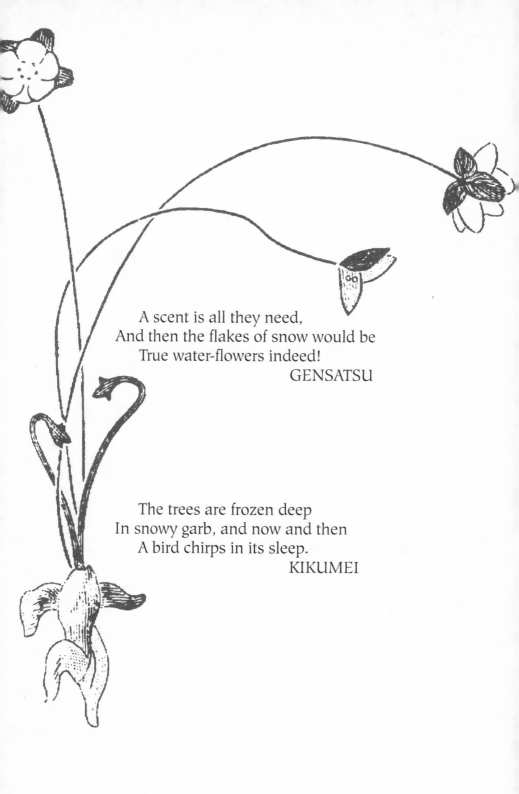

A scent is all they need,
And then the flakes of snow would be
True water-flowers indeed!
                    GENSATSU

The trees are frozen deep
In snowy garb, and now and then
A bird chirps in its sleep.
                    KIKUMEI

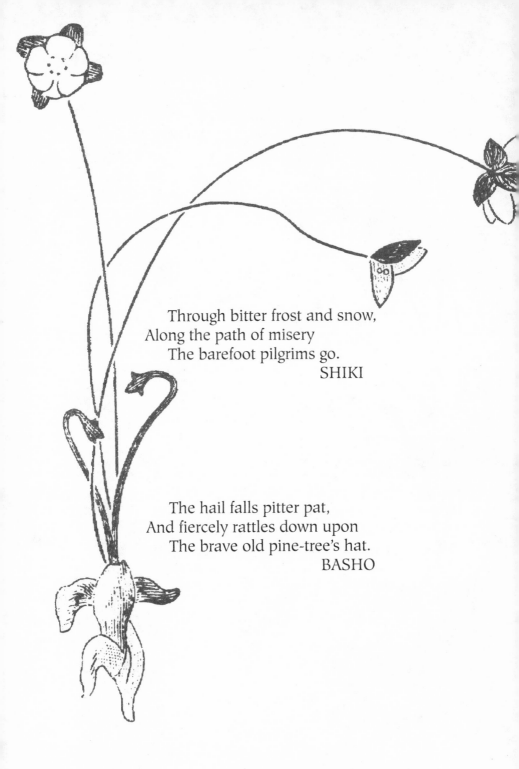

Through bitter frost and snow,
Along the path of misery
The barefoot pilgrims go.
SHIKI

The hail falls pitter pat,
And fiercely rattles down upon
The brave old pine-tree's hat.
BASHO

'Tis winter time, and now
The sun peeps out a moment, just
To make a formal bow.

KITO

Now all the world is white,
But where is one to find a spot
To view the lovely sight?

RIU

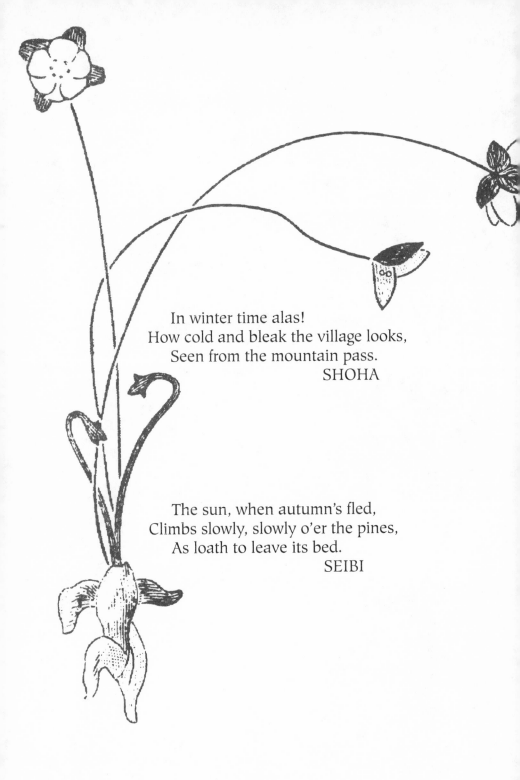

In winter time alas!
How cold and bleak the village looks,
Seen from the mountain pass.
SHOHA

The sun, when autumn's fled,
Climbs slowly, slowly o'er the pines,
As loath to leave its bed.
SEIBI

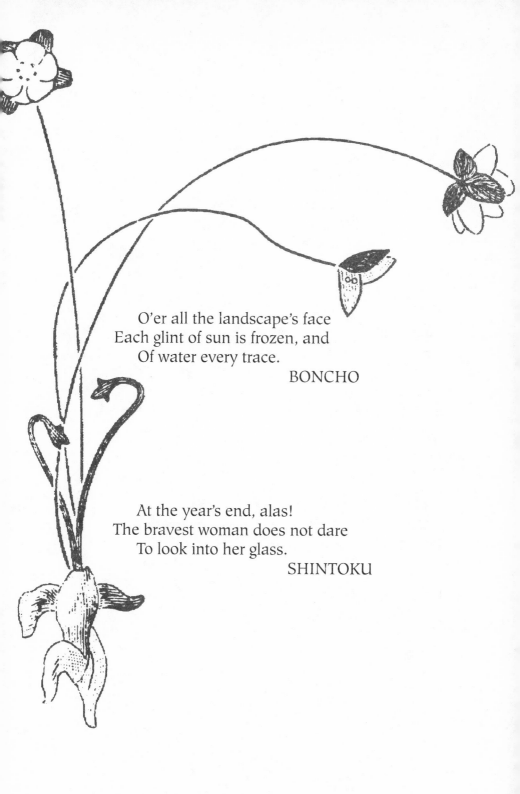

O'er all the landscape's face
Each glint of sun is frozen, and
Of water every trace.

BONCHO

At the year's end, alas!
The bravest woman does not dare
To look into her glass.

SHINTOKU

Another year has flown;
I must not let my parents see
How gray my hair has grown.
ETSUJIN

Now the New Year draws on,
But soon, alas! The coming year
Will be the year that's gone.
ROSEN

The year is nearly o'er,
And it will do me good to see
The plums in bloom once more.
BASHO

A dance will clear away
The troubles of the year that's flown,
But sing no songs to-day.
TATSE

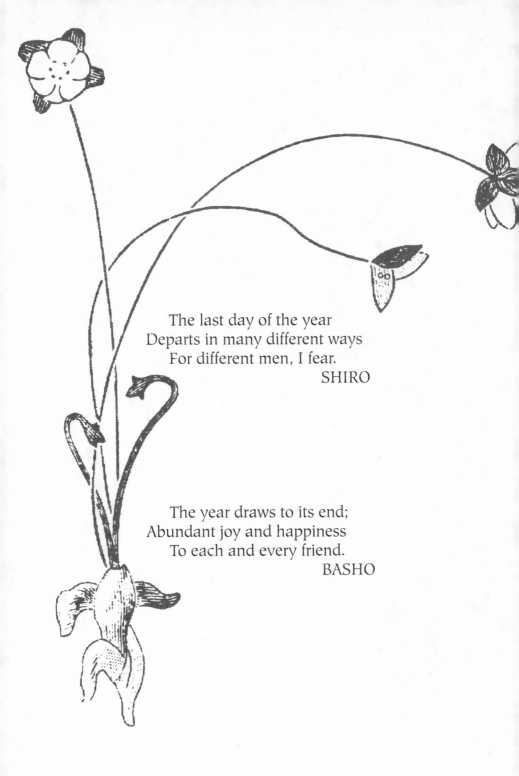

The last day of the year
Departs in many different ways
For different men, I fear.
SHIRO

The year draws to its end;
Abundant joy and happiness
To each and every friend.
BASHO

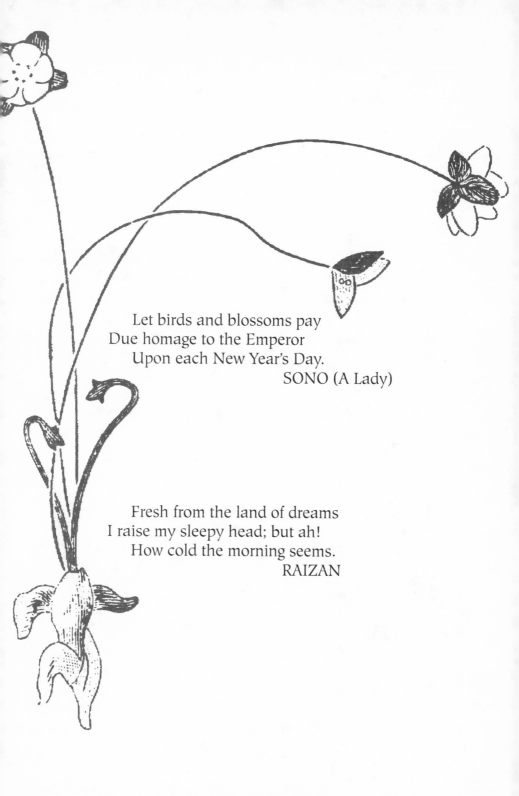

Let birds and blossoms pay
Due homage to the Emperor
Upon each New Year's Day.
SONO (A Lady)

Fresh from the land of dreams
I raise my sleepy head; but ah!
How cold the morning seems.
RAIZAN

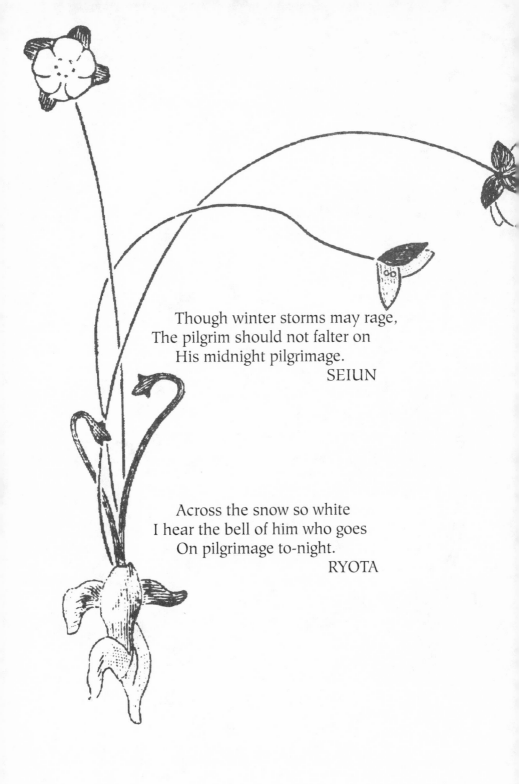

Though winter storms may rage,
The pilgrim should not falter on
His midnight pilgrimage.
                    SEIUN

Across the snow so white
I hear the bell of him who goes
On pilgrimage to-night.
                    RYOTA

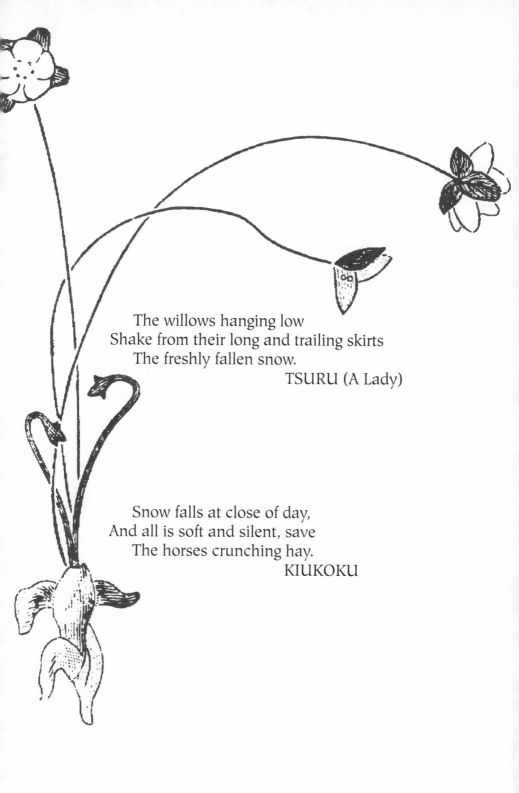

The willows hanging low
Shake from their long and trailing skirts
The freshly fallen snow.
　　　　　　　TSURU (A Lady)

Snow falls at close of day,
And all is soft and silent, save
The horses crunching hay.
　　　　　　　KIUKOKU

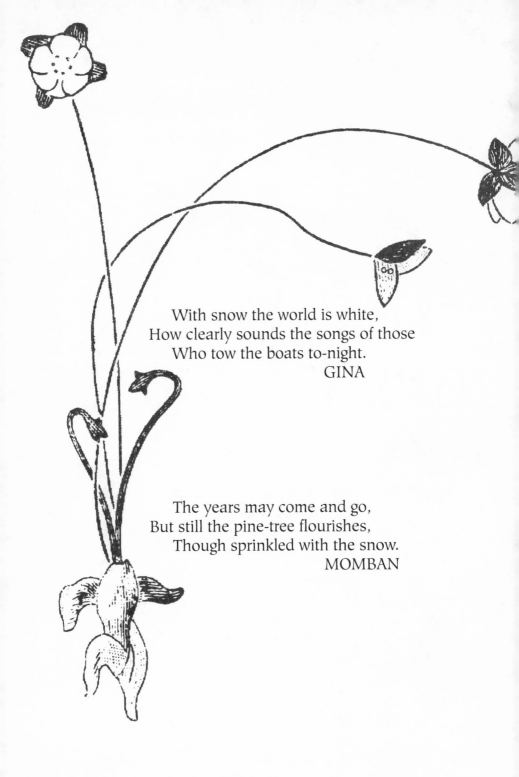

With snow the world is white,
How clearly sounds the songs of those
Who tow the boats to-night.
                    GINA

The years may come and go,
But still the pine-tree flourishes,
Though sprinkled with the snow.
                    MOMBAN

The day breaks cold and drear,
And in the ashes of my hearth
A cricket's chirp I hear.
TANDAN

The night is scarce begun,
And yet I hear a voice that says,
'The charcoal is all done!'
SEIBI

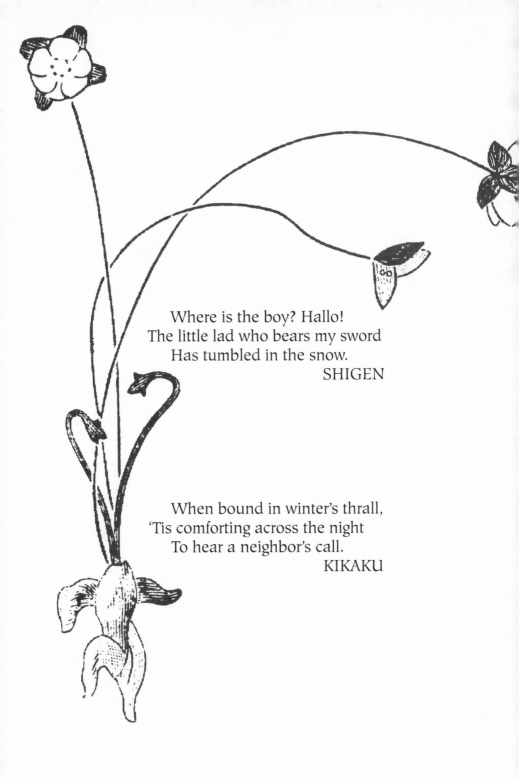

Where is the boy? Hallo!
The little lad who bears my sword
Has tumbled in the snow.
          SHIGEN

When bound in winter's thrall,
'Tis comforting across the night
To hear a neighbor's call.
          KIKAKU

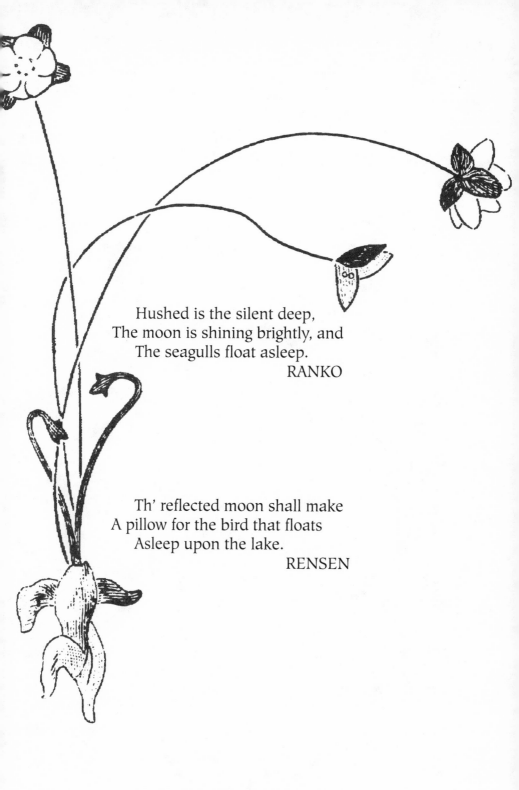

Hushed is the silent deep,
The moon is shining brightly, and
The seagulls float asleep.
                    RANKO

Th' reflected moon shall make
A pillow for the bird that floats
Asleep upon the lake.
                    RENSEN

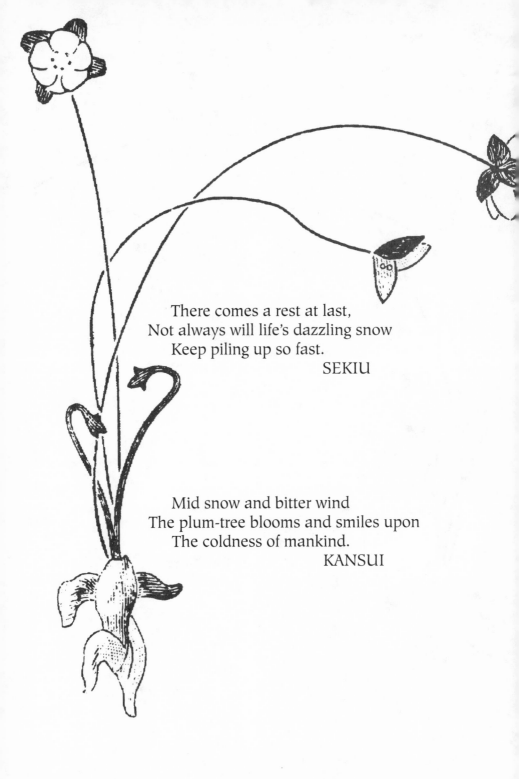

There comes a rest at last,
Not always will life's dazzling snow
Keep piling up so fast.
                    SEKIU

Mid snow and bitter wind
The plum-tree blooms and smiles upon
The coldness of mankind.
                    KANSUI

I came to look, and lo!
The plum-tree petals scatter down,
A fall of purest snow.

RANKO

This temple still can show
Saved by the shadow of the trees.
A little patch of snow.

RENGETSU

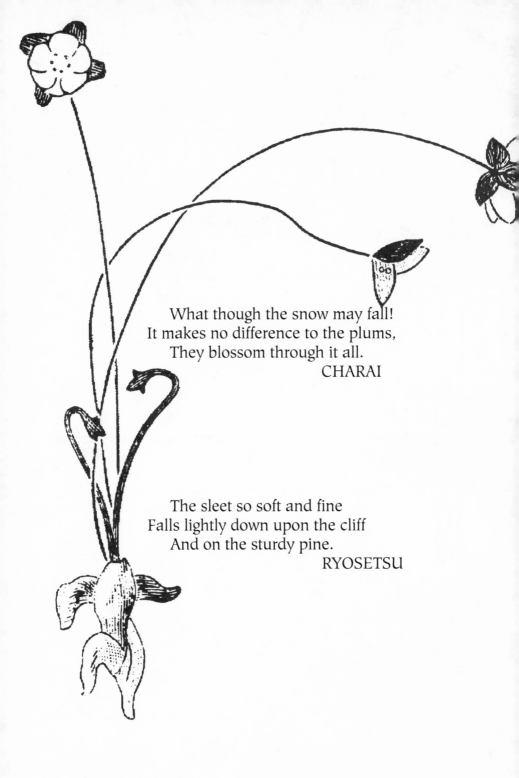

What though the snow may fall!
It makes no difference to the plums,
They blossom through it all.
                    CHARAI

The sleet so soft and fine
Falls lightly down upon the cliff
And on the sturdy pine.
                    RYOSETSU

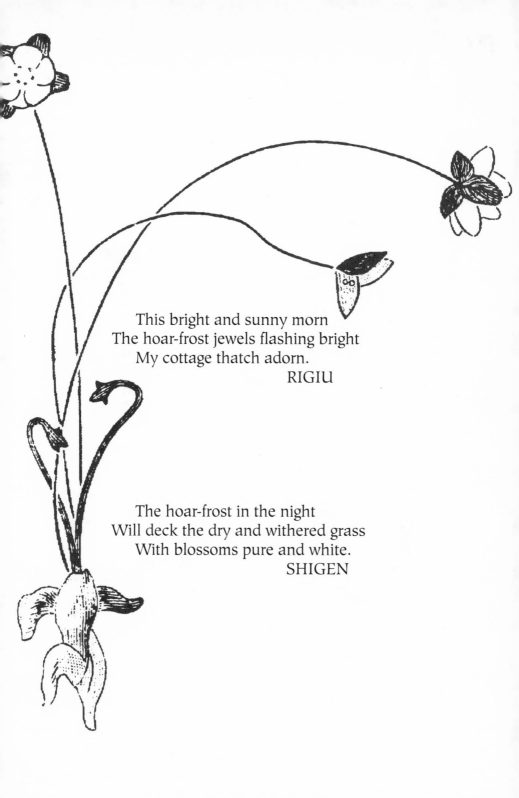

This bright and sunny morn
The hoar-frost jewels flashing bright
My cottage thatch adorn.
                    RIGIU

The hoar-frost in the night
Will deck the dry and withered grass
With blossoms pure and white.
                    SHIGEN

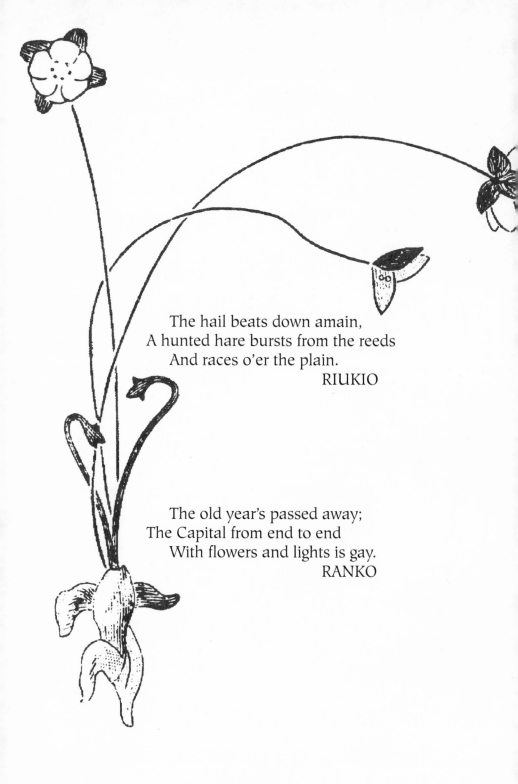

The hail beats down amain,
A hunted hare bursts from the reeds
And races o'er the plain.

RIUKIO

The old year's passed away;
The Capital from end to end
With flowers and lights is gay.

RANKO

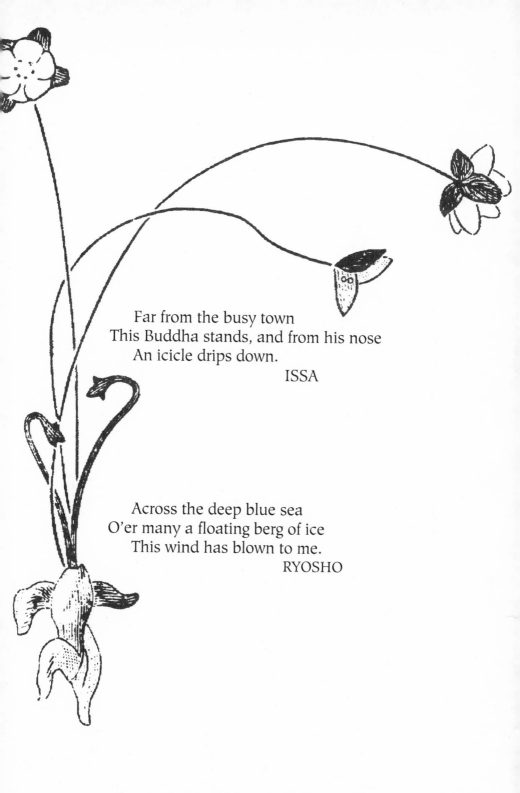

Far from the busy town
This Buddha stands, and from his nose
An icicle drips down.

ISSA

Across the deep blue sea
O'er many a floating berg of ice
This wind has blown to me.

RYOSHO

SPRING

春

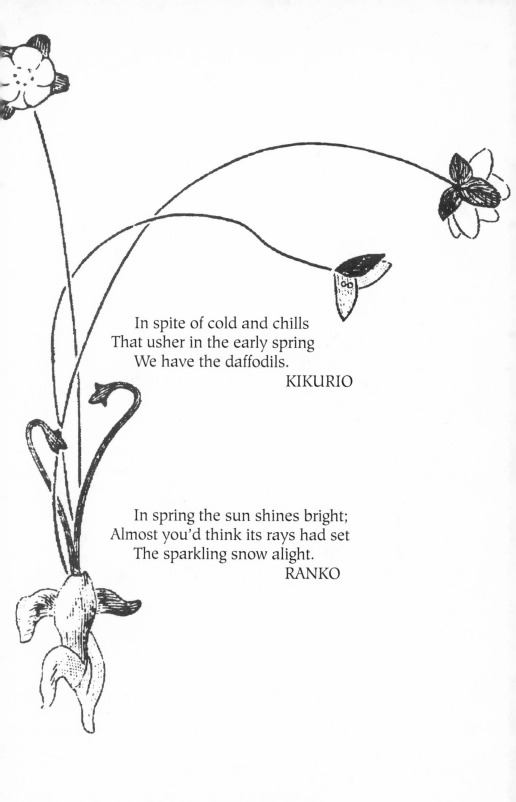

In spite of cold and chills
That usher in the early spring
We have the daffodils.
                    KIKURIO

In spring the sun shines bright;
Almost you'd think its rays had set
The sparkling snow alight.
                    RANKO

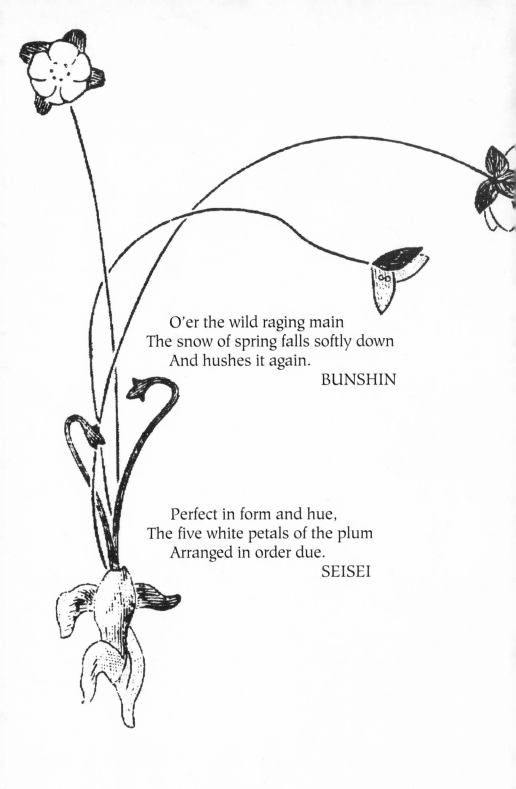

O'er the wild raging main
The snow of spring falls softly down
And hushes it again.

BUNSHIN

Perfect in form and hue,
The five white petals of the plum
Arranged in order due.

SEISEI

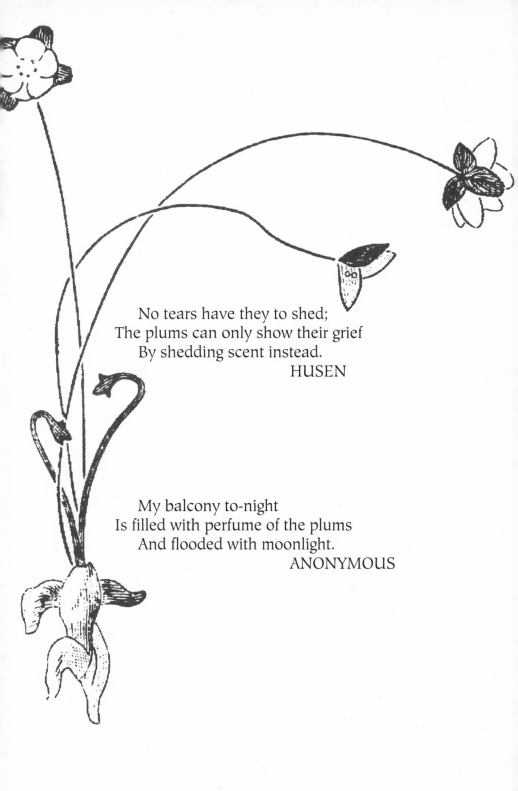

No tears have they to shed;
The plums can only show their grief
By shedding scent instead.
                    HUSEN

My balcony to-night
Is filled with perfume of the plums
And flooded with moonlight.
                    ANONYMOUS

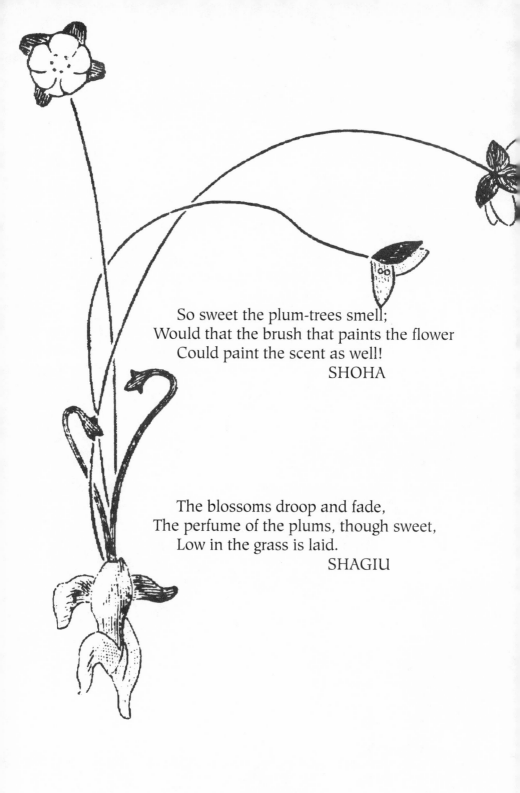

So sweet the plum-trees smell;
Would that the brush that paints the flower
Could paint the scent as well!
SHOHA

The blossoms droop and fade,
The perfume of the plums, though sweet,
Low in the grass is laid.
SHAGIU

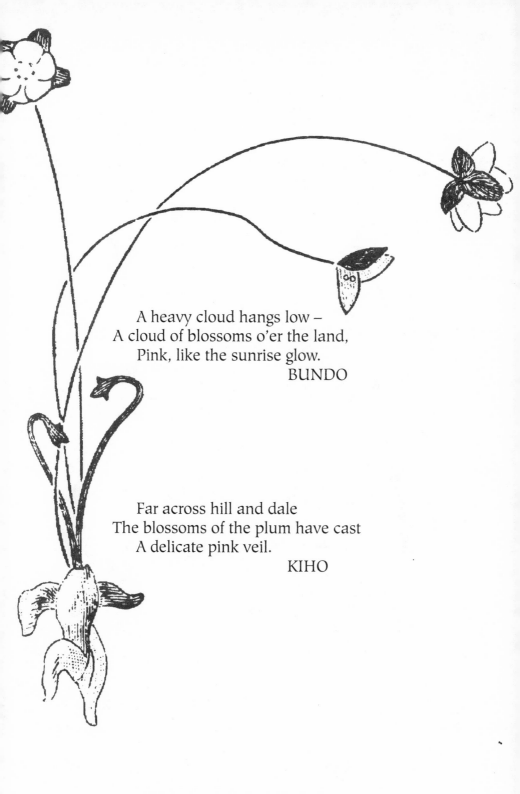

A heavy cloud hangs low –
A cloud of blossoms o'er the land,
Pink, like the sunrise glow.
BUNDO

Far across hill and dale
The blossoms of the plum have cast
A delicate pink veil.
KIHO

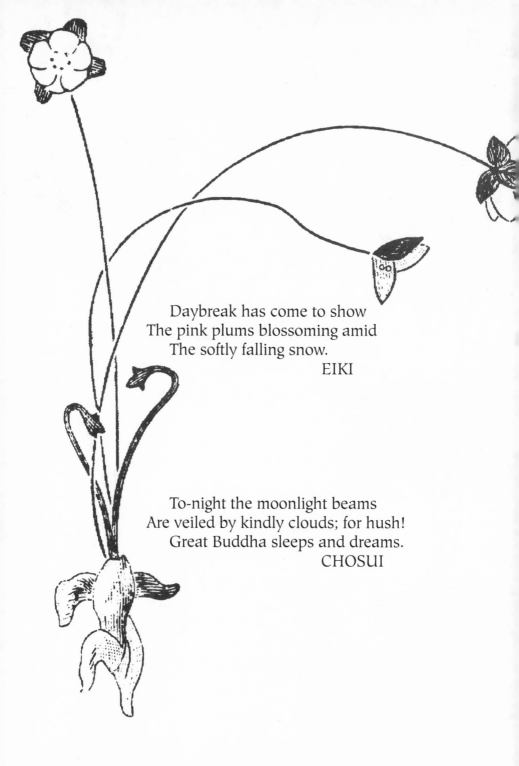

Daybreak has come to show
The pink plums blossoming amid
The softly falling snow.
                    EIKI

To-night the moonlight beams
Are veiled by kindly clouds; for hush!
Great Buddha sleeps and dreams.
                    CHOSUI

When the bright moon above
Can scarcely pierce the shady pines,
That is the dusk I love.
                    KIKAKU

When clouds drive o'er the moon,
Too quickly flies the lovely night,
The morning comes too soon.
                    KODO

So peacefully live I,
I scarcely heed how rapidly
The days and months slip by.
TAIGI

The evening mist hangs low,
And through the cross-beams of the bridge
The slanting sunbeams show.
HOKUSHI

The mists close round about
The holy Buddhist temple, and
The sunset bell rings out.
                    UNGIO

The crimson sunset glow
Is on the mountain, on the mist,
And on the sea below.
                    RANKO

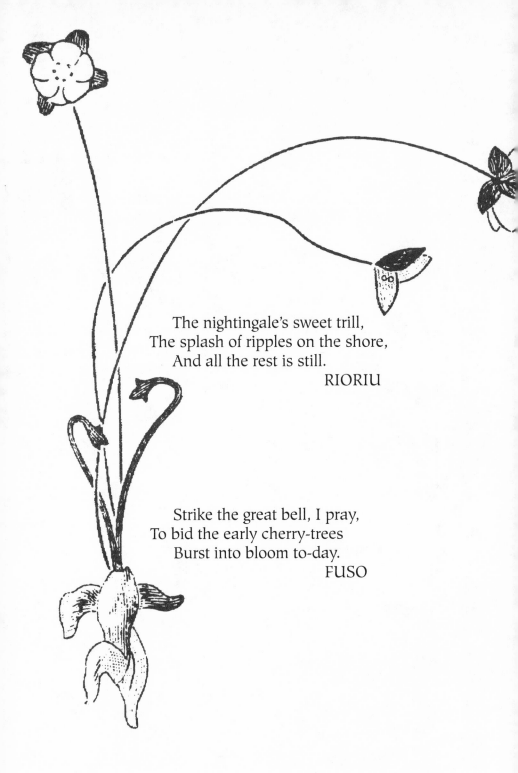

The nightingale's sweet trill,
The splash of ripples on the shore,
  And all the rest is still.

                    RIORIU

Strike the great bell, I pray,
To bid the early cherry-trees
  Burst into bloom to-day.

                    FUSO

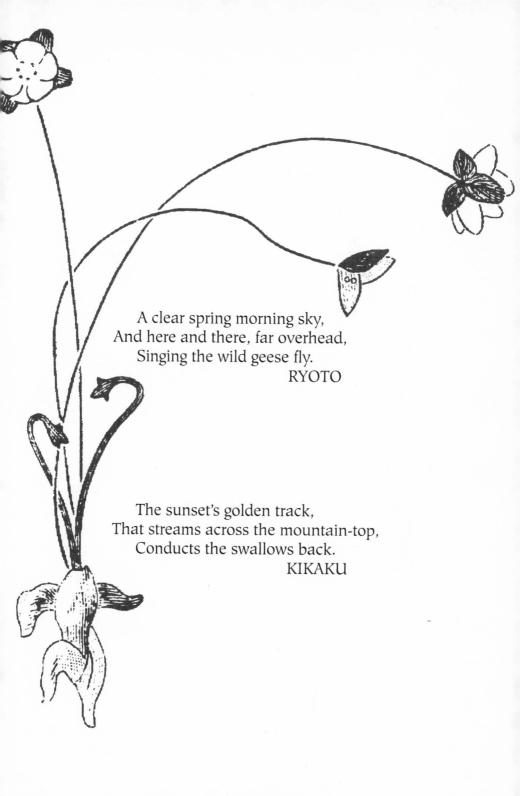

A clear spring morning sky,
And here and there, far overhead,
Singing the wild geese fly.
                    RYOTO

The sunset's golden track,
That streams across the mountain-top,
Conducts the swallows back.
                    KIKAKU

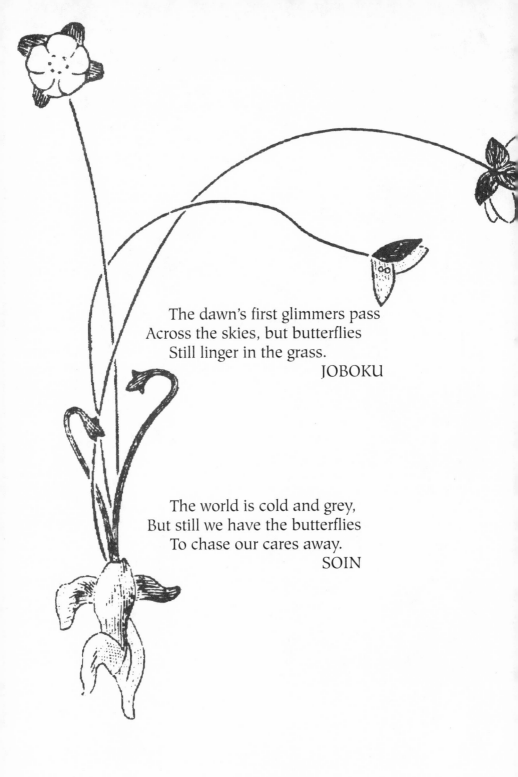

The dawn's first glimmers pass
Across the skies, but butterflies
Still linger in the grass.
JOBOKU

The world is cold and grey,
But still we have the butterflies
To chase our cares away.
SOIN

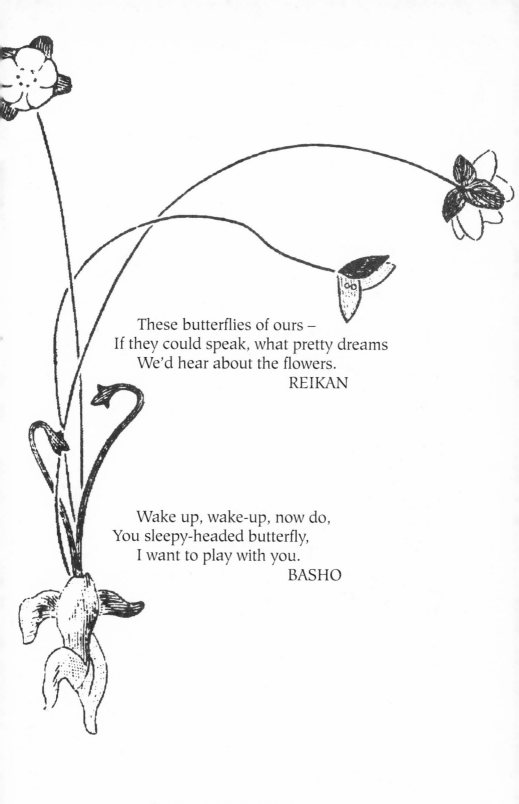

These butterflies of ours –
If they could speak, what pretty dreams
We'd hear about the flowers.
REIKAN

Wake up, wake-up, now do,
You sleepy-headed butterfly,
I want to play with you.
BASHO

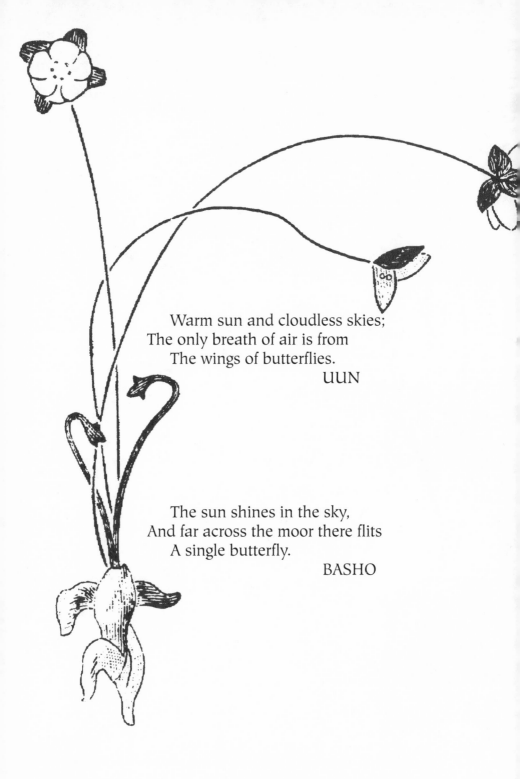

Warm sun and cloudless skies;
The only breath of air is from
The wings of butterflies.

UUN

The sun shines in the sky,
And far across the moor there flits
A single butterfly.

BASHO

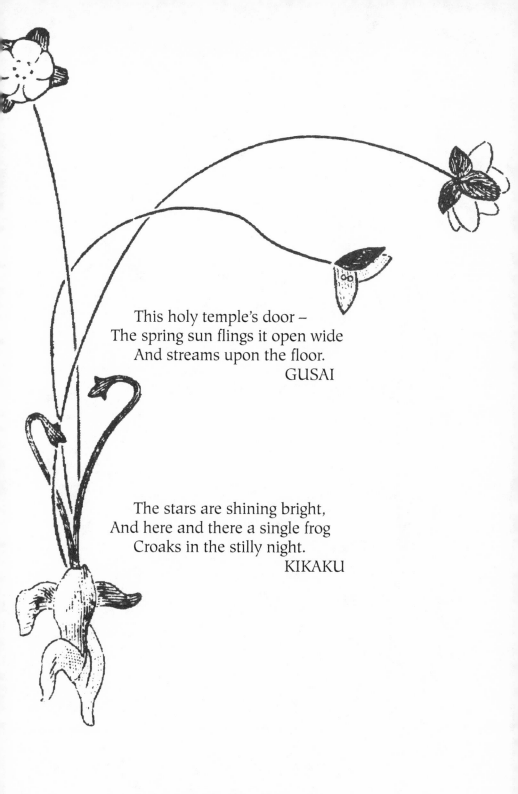

This holy temple's door –
The spring sun flings it open wide
And streams upon the floor.
GUSAI

The stars are shining bright,
And here and there a single frog
Croaks in the stilly night.
KIKAKU

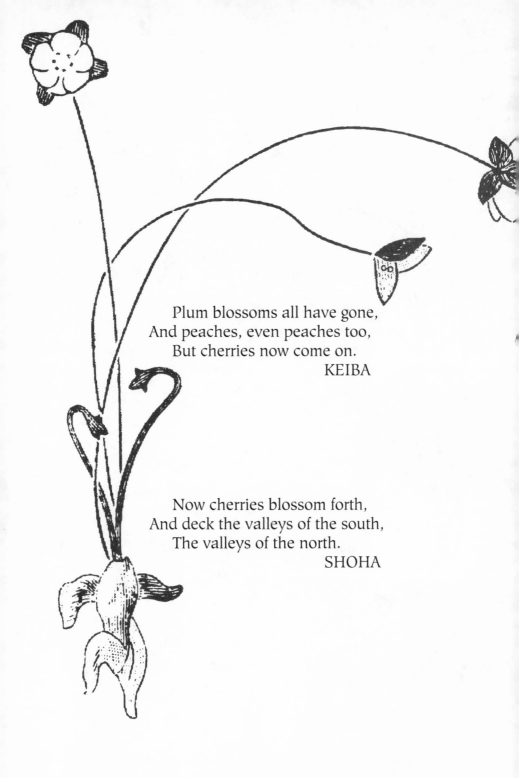

Plum blossoms all have gone,
And peaches, even peaches too,
But cherries now come on.
                    KEIBA

Now cherries blossom forth,
And deck the valleys of the south,
The valleys of the north.
                    SHOHA

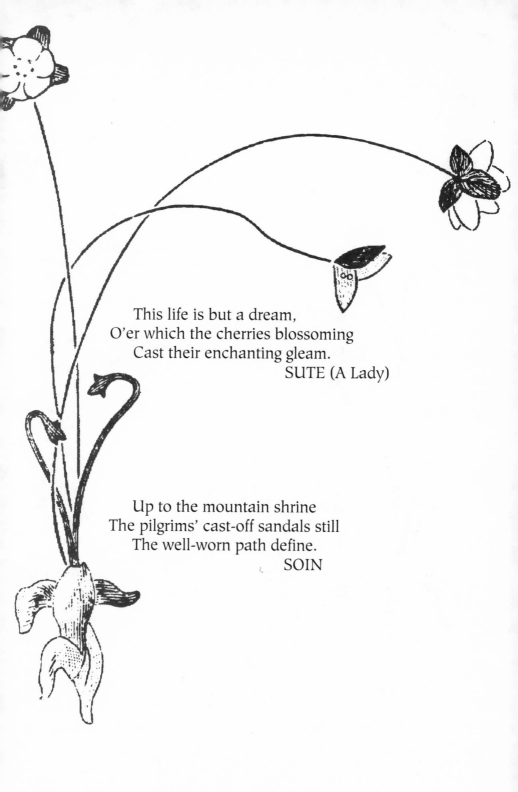

This life is but a dream,
O'er which the cherries blossoming
Cast their enchanting gleam.
                    SUTE (A Lady)

Up to the mountain shrine
The pilgrims' cast-off sandals still
The well-worn path define.
                    SOIN

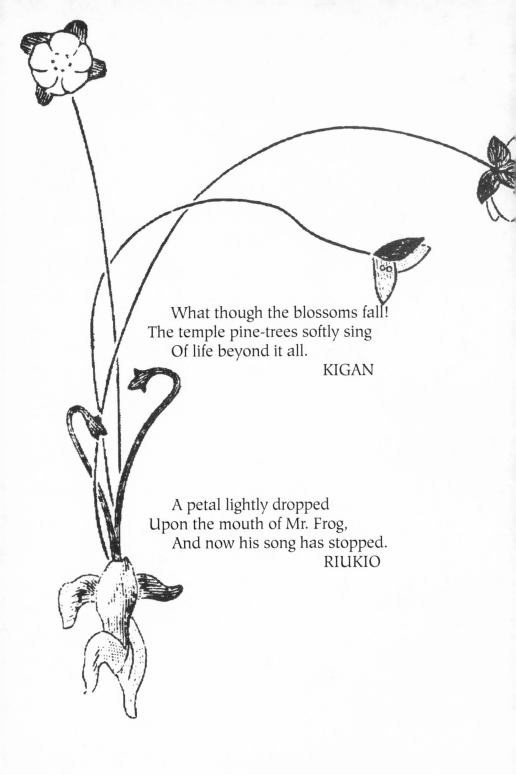

What though the blossoms fall!
The temple pine-trees softly sing
Of life beyond it all.
                    KIGAN

A petal lightly dropped
Upon the mouth of Mr. Frog,
        And now his song has stopped.
                    RIUKIO

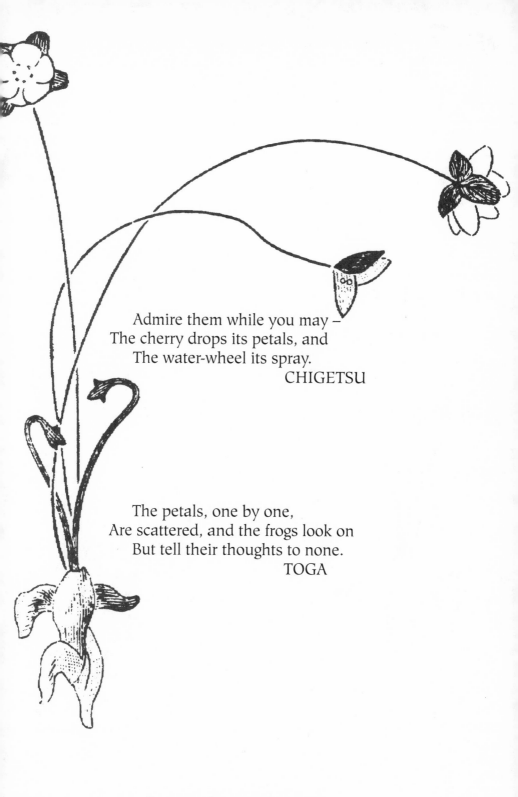

Admire them while you may –
The cherry drops its petals, and
The water-wheel its spray.
CHIGETSU

The petals, one by one,
Are scattered, and the frogs look on
But tell their thoughts to none.
TOGA

'Tis true the blossoms grow
'Tis true we see their beauty, and
'Tis true they quickly go.
ONITSURA

To-day I tramp along
In silence, for no hymn of mine
Could match the spring wind's song.
RYOTA

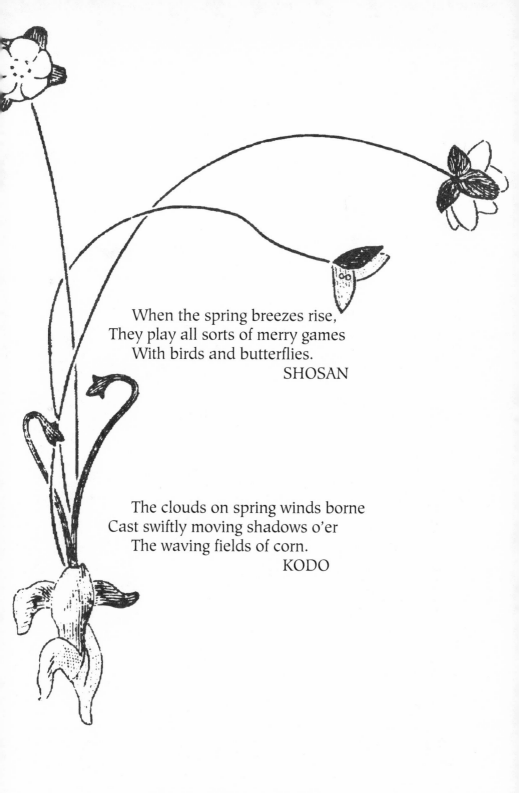

When the spring breezes rise,
They play all sorts of merry games
With birds and butterflies.
SHOSAN

The clouds on spring winds borne
Cast swiftly moving shadows o'er
The waving fields of corn.
KODO

The bells at sunset ring,
And evening brings a gentle shower,
The welcome shower of spring.
MIYOSHI

Here the late cherry grows,
And bubbling o'er its pebble bed
A little streamlet flows.
GANSHU

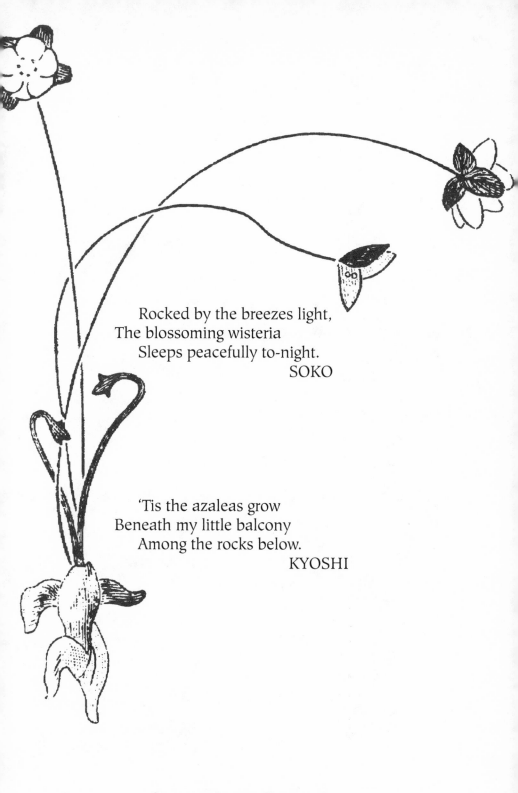

Rocked by the breezes light,
The blossoming wisteria
Sleeps peacefully to-night.
SOKO

'Tis the azaleas grow
Beneath my little balcony
Among the rocks below.
KYOSHI

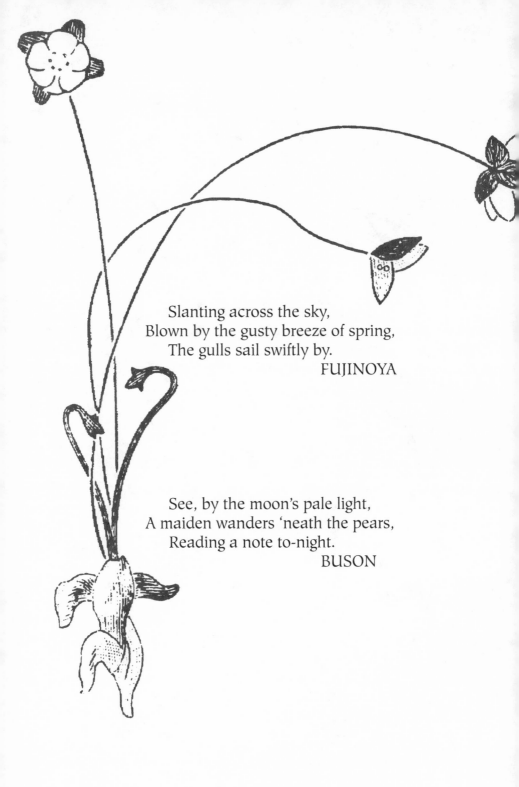

Slanting across the sky,
Blown by the gusty breeze of spring,
The gulls sail swiftly by.
                              FUJINOYA

See, by the moon's pale light,
A maiden wanders 'neath the pears,
Reading a note to-night.
                              BUSON

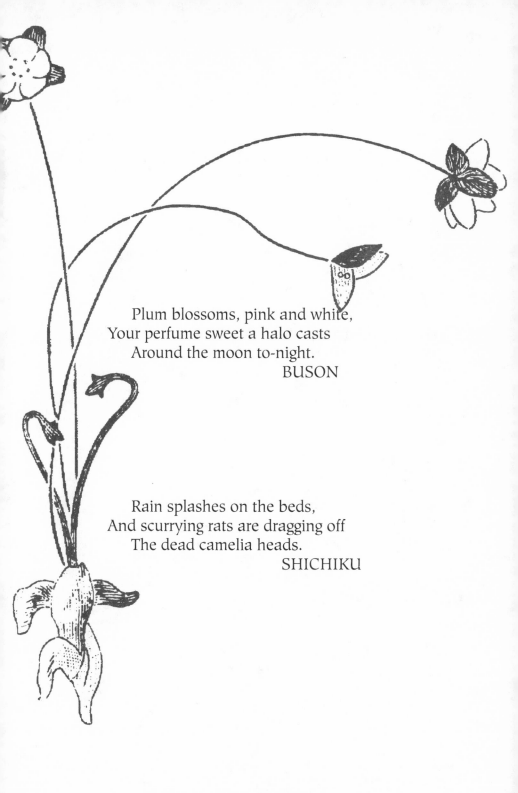

Plum blossoms, pink and white,
Your perfume sweet a halo casts
Around the moon to-night.
                    BUSON

Rain splashes on the beds,
And scurrying rats are dragging off
The dead camelia heads.
                    SHICHIKU

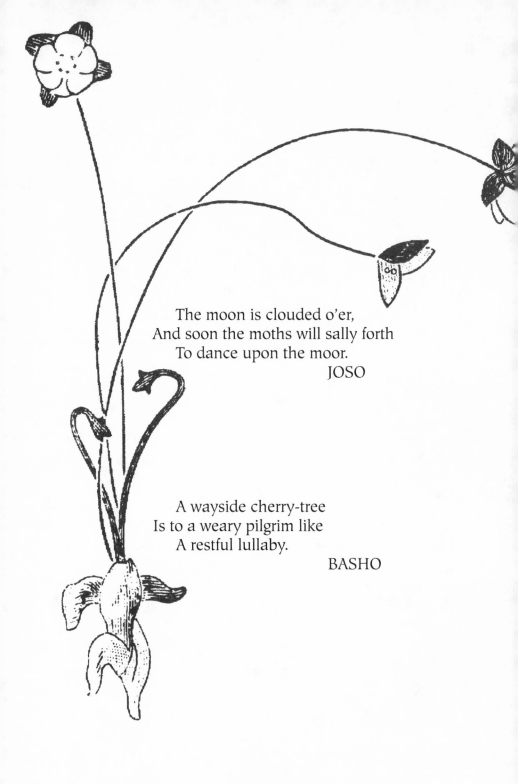

The moon is clouded o'er,
And soon the moths will sally forth
To dance upon the moor.
JOSO

A wayside cherry-tree
Is to a weary pilgrim like
A restful lullaby.

BASHO

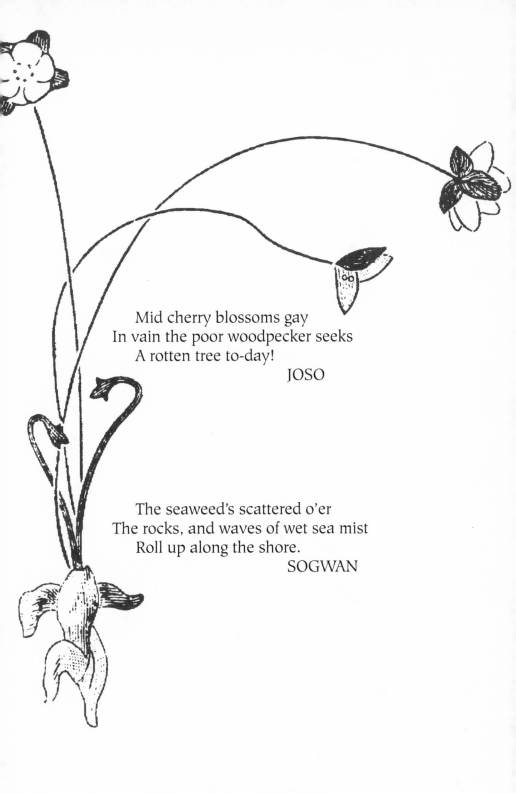

Mid cherry blossoms gay
In vain the poor woodpecker seeks
A rotten tree to-day!
                    JOSO

The seaweed's scattered o'er
The rocks, and waves of wet sea mist
Roll up along the shore.
                    SOGWAN

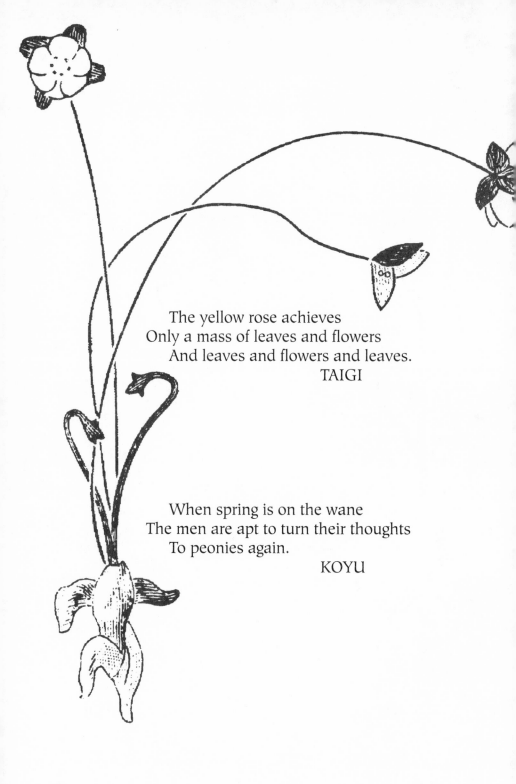

The yellow rose achieves
Only a mass of leaves and flowers
And leaves and flowers and leaves.
TAIGI

When spring is on the wane
The men are apt to turn their thoughts
To peonies again.
KOYU

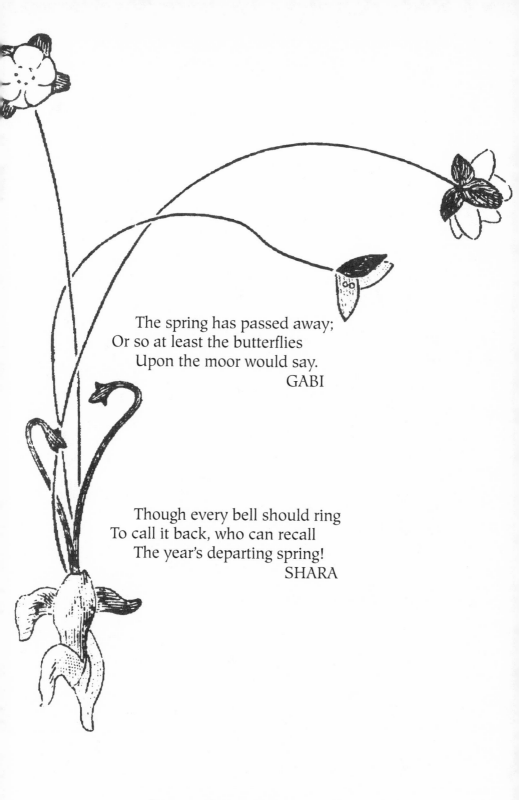

The spring has passed away;
Or so at least the butterflies
Upon the moor would say.
GABI

Though every bell should ring
To call it back, who can recall
The year's departing spring!
SHARA

SUMMER

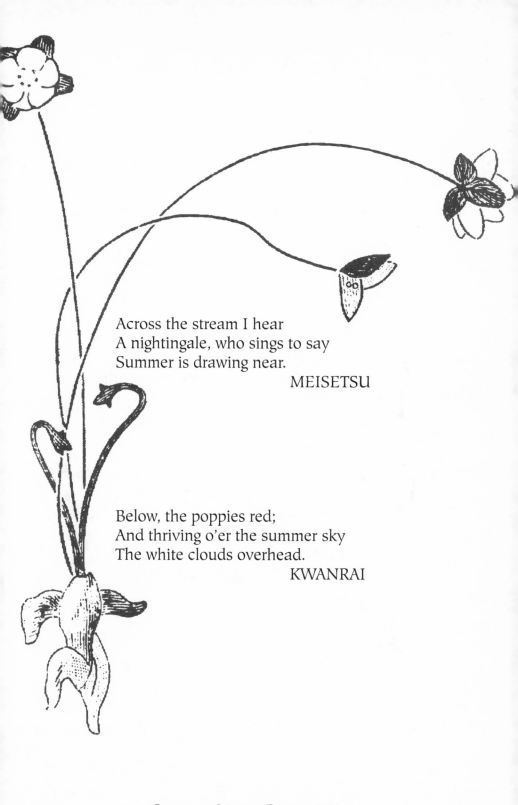

Across the stream I hear
A nightingale, who sings to say
Summer is drawing near.
                    MEISETSU

Below, the poppies red;
And thriving o'er the summer sky
The white clouds overhead.
                    KWANRAI

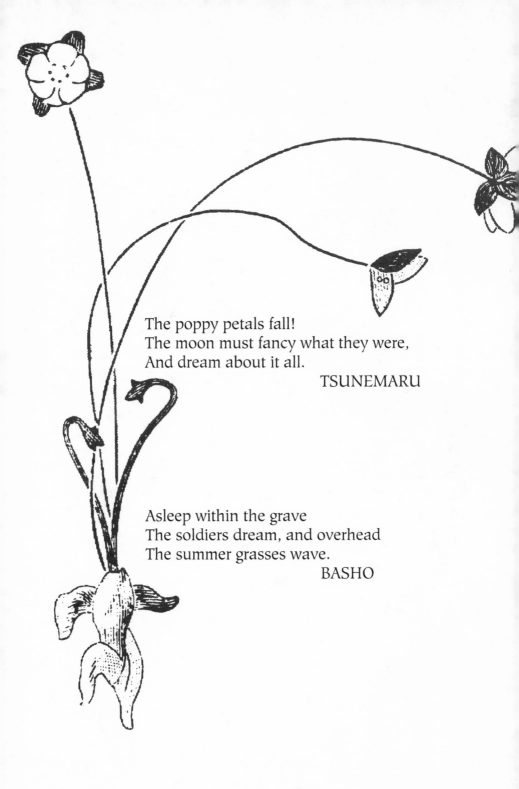

The poppy petals fall!
The moon must fancy what they were,
And dream about it all.
                    TSUNEMARU

Asleep within the grave
The soldiers dream, and overhead
The summer grasses wave.
                    BASHO

The woodcutter has gone,
And while the cuckoo sings alone
The shades of night draw on.
                    KOZAN

The cuckoo's song is given
Even to thieves who prowl at night, –
A precious gift from heaven.
                    SOOKU

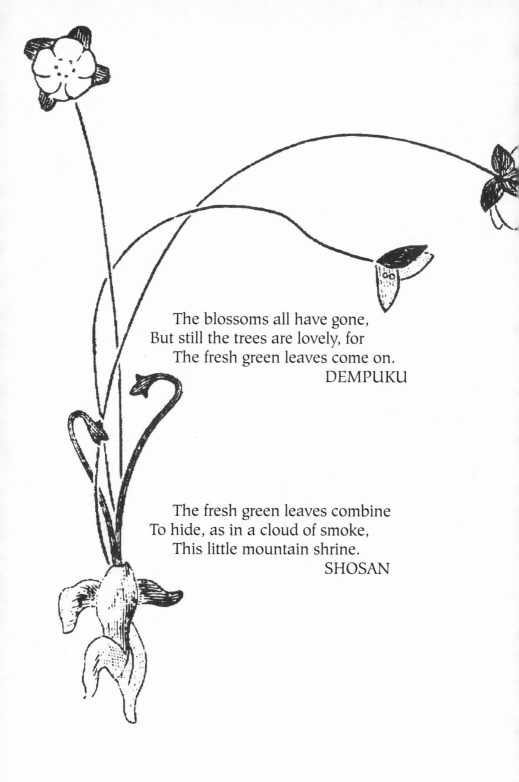

The blossoms all have gone,
But still the trees are lovely, for
The fresh green leaves come on.
                    DEMPUKU

The fresh green leaves combine
To hide, as in a cloud of smoke,
This little mountain shrine.
                    SHOSAN

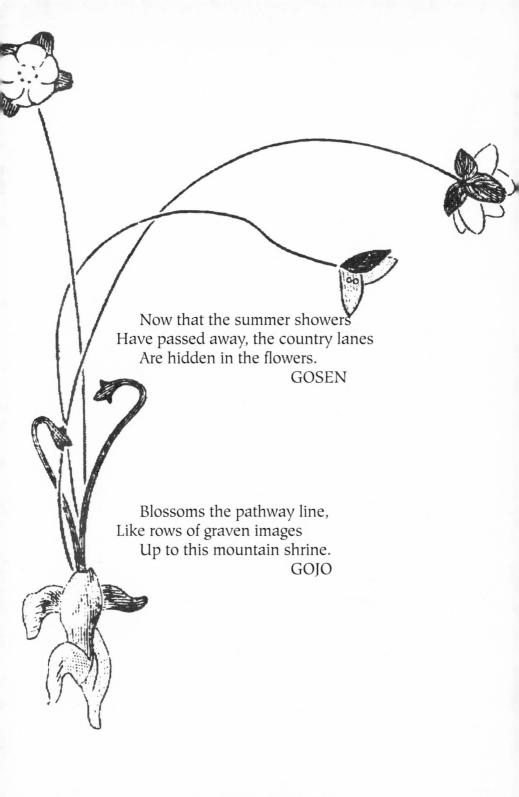

Now that the summer showers
Have passed away, the country lanes
Are hidden in the flowers.
GOSEN

Blossoms the pathway line,
Like rows of graven images
Up to this mountain shrine.
GOJO

No rose could ever rue
The exquisite embroidery
Of sparkling drops of dew.
                RIUMIN

This crystal water's flow
Shall lead you gently on to where
The flow'ring mosses grow.
                KAKO

In summer sleep is vain;
I barely close my eyelids when
'Tis time to wake again.
                    IRIU

This lovely summer morn
Hushed is the voice of every man
In wonder at the dawn.
                    RYOTA

Ere yet the sun is high,
All blue the iris blossoms wave,
The color of the sky.

GASETSU

Down from her dainty head
The Lily Princess lightly drops
A spider's airy thread.

SORIO

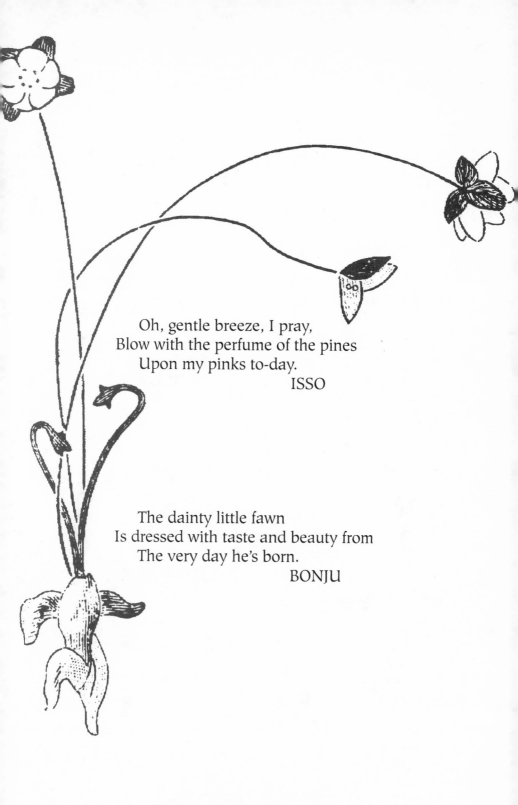

Oh, gentle breeze, I pray,
Blow with the perfume of the pines
Upon my pinks to-day.

ISSO

The dainty little fawn
Is dressed with taste and beauty from
The very day he's born.

BONJU

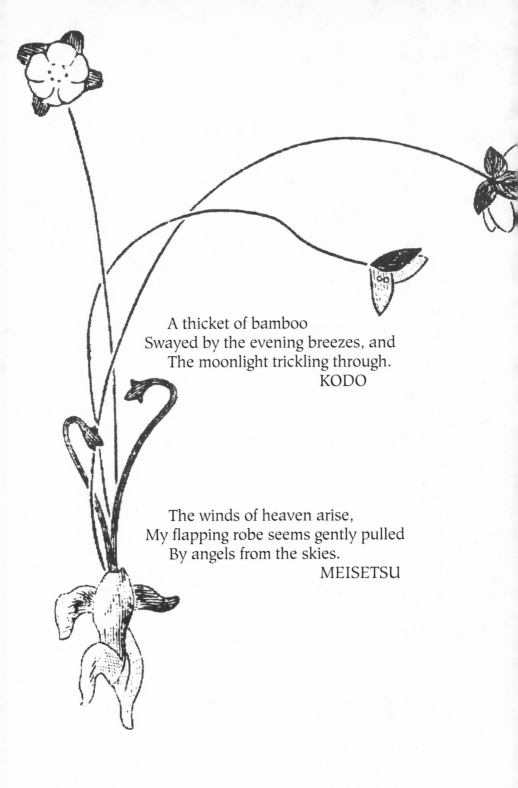

A thicket of bamboo
Swayed by the evening breezes, and
The moonlight trickling through.
KODO

The winds of heaven arise,
My flapping robe seems gently pulled
By angels from the skies.
MEISETSU

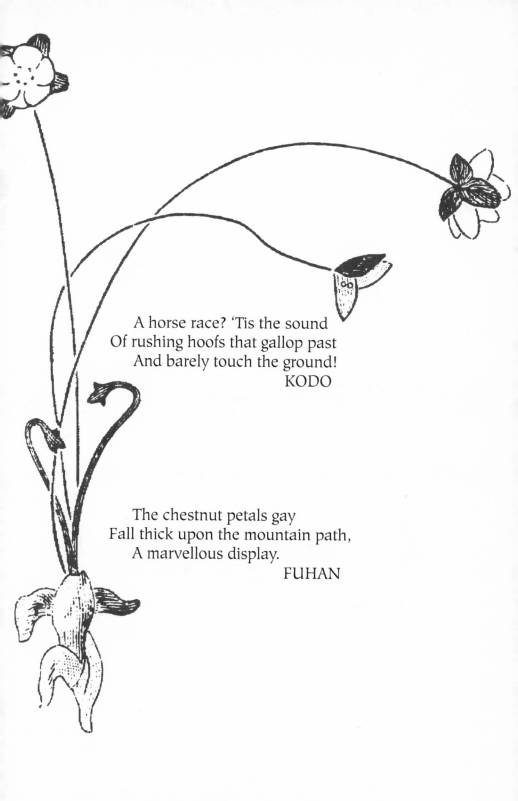

A horse race? 'Tis the sound
Of rushing hoofs that gallop past
And barely touch the ground!
KODO

The chestnut petals gay
Fall thick upon the mountain path,
A marvellous display.
FUHAN

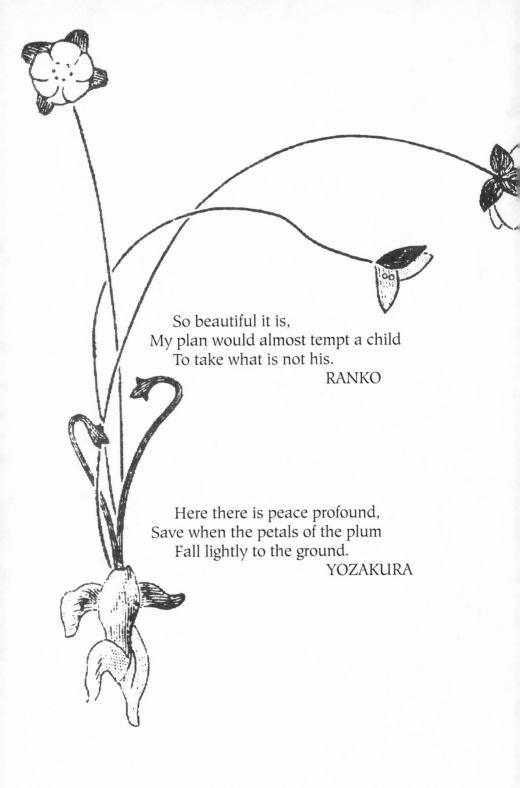

So beautiful it is,
My plan would almost tempt a child
To take what is not his.
                    RANKO

Here there is peace profound,
Save when the petals of the plum
Fall lightly to the ground.
                    YOZAKURA

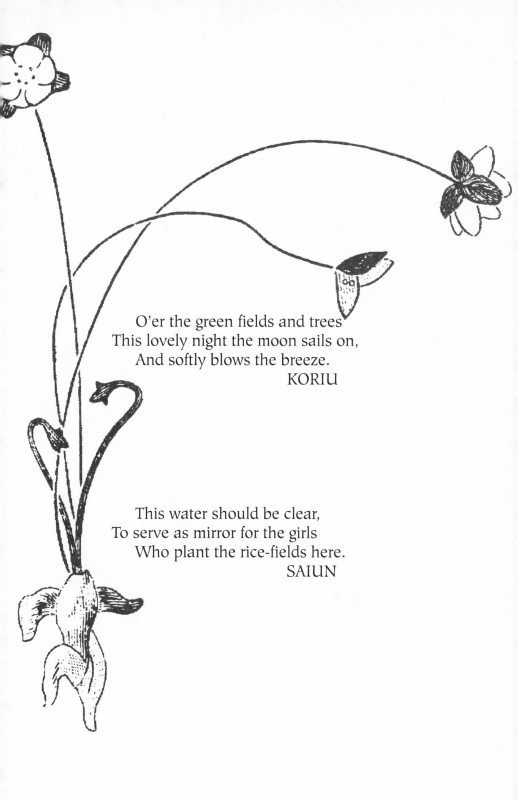

O'er the green fields and trees
This lovely night the moon sails on,
And softly blows the breeze.
                    KORIU

This water should be clear,
To serve as mirror for the girls
Who plant the rice-fields here.
                    SAIUN

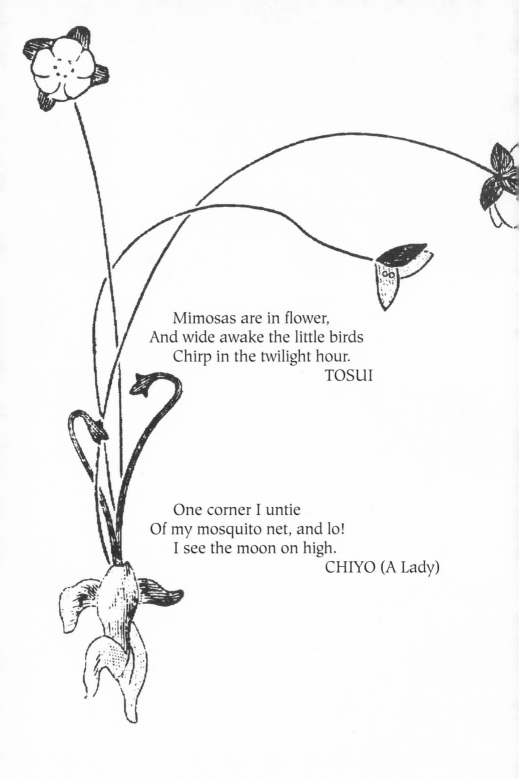

Mimosas are in flower,
And wide awake the little birds
Chirp in the twilight hour.
TOSUI

One corner I untie
Of my mosquito net, and lo!
I see the moon on high.
CHIYO (A Lady)

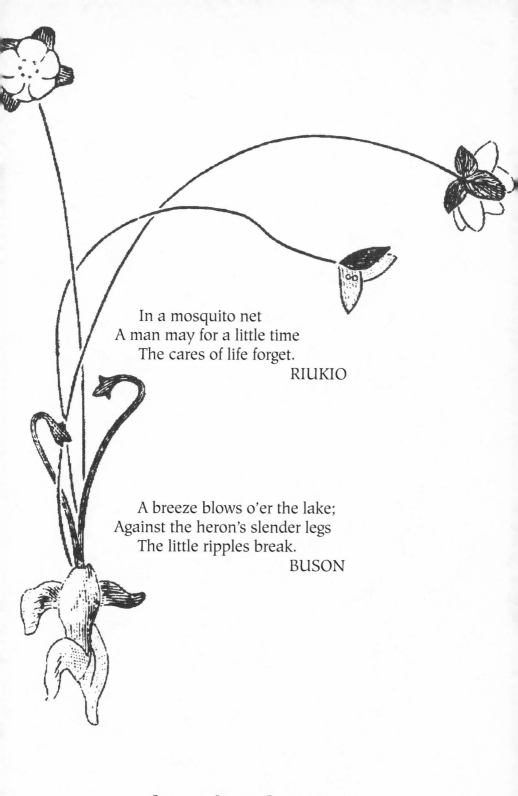

In a mosquito net
A man may for a little time
The cares of life forget.
                    RIUKIO

A breeze blows o'er the lake;
Against the heron's slender legs
The little ripples break.
                    BUSON

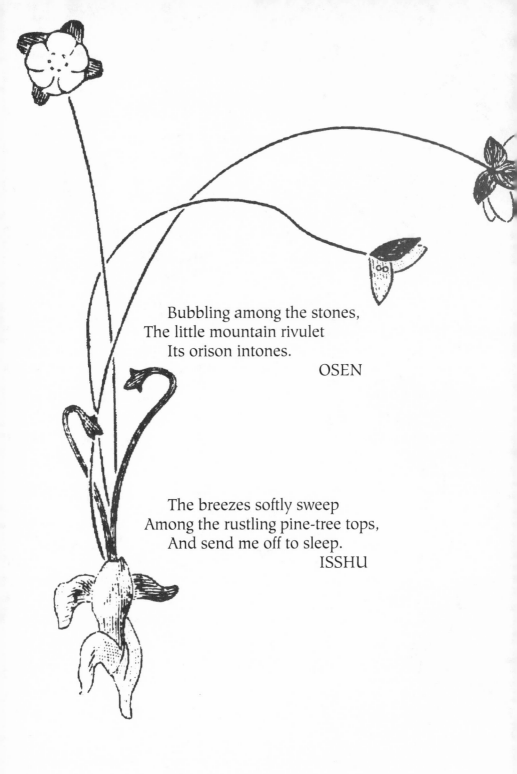

Bubbling among the stones,
The little mountain rivulet
Its orison intones.
OSEN

The breezes softly sweep
Among the rustling pine-tree tops,
And send me off to sleep.
ISSHU

The sunlit waters gleam,
And worshippers with solemn rites
Wash in the shallow stream.
HEKIGODO

Oh peaceful summer days,
When on the hills the birds sing forth
Their melody of praise.
SHOHA

I've wandered on to-night,
Till now I see the summer moon
Sink sideways out of sight.
BUKAKU

Oh summer moon, we pray,
Open the wind-bag of the Gods
And let the zephyrs play.
KISEN

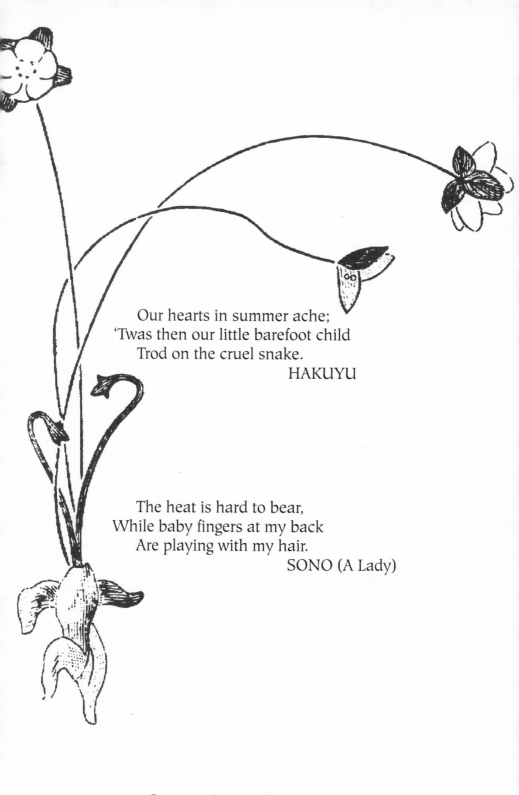

Our hearts in summer ache;
'Twas then our little barefoot child
Trod on the cruel snake.
                    HAKUYU

The heat is hard to bear,
While baby fingers at my back
Are playing with my hair.
                    SONO (A Lady)

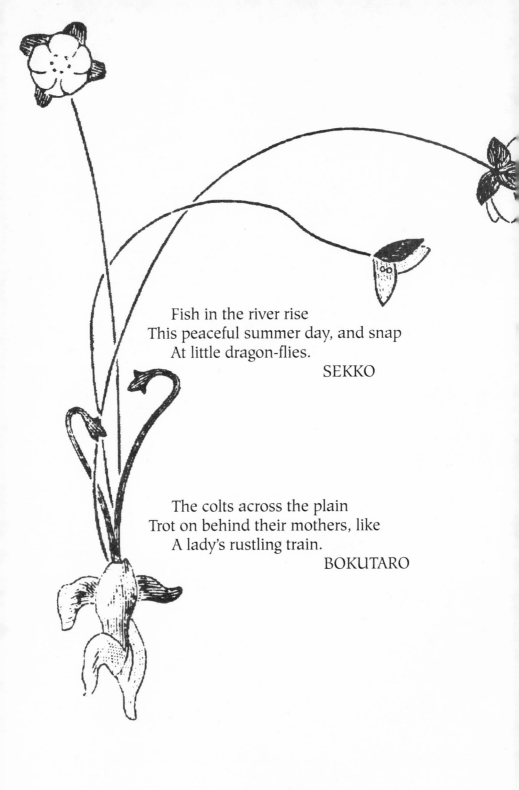

Fish in the river rise
This peaceful summer day, and snap
At little dragon-flies.
                    SEKKO

The colts across the plain
Trot on behind their mothers, like
A lady's rustling train.
                    BOKUTARO

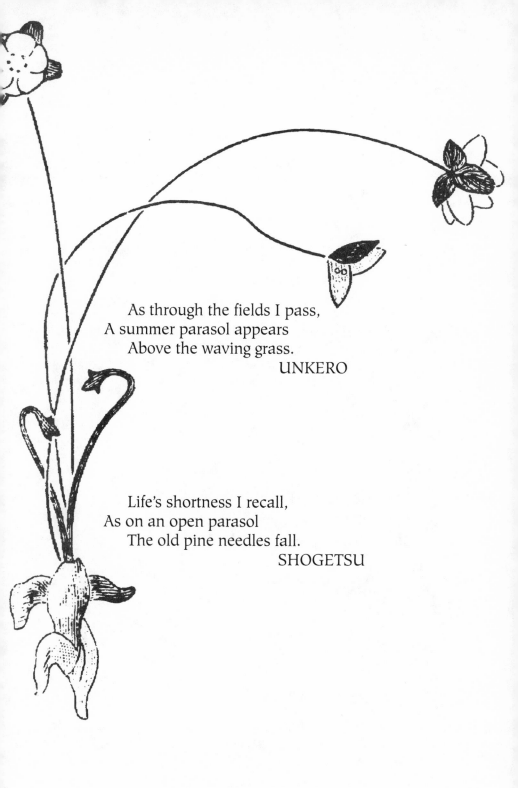

As through the fields I pass,
A summer parasol appears
Above the waving grass.
UNKERO

Life's shortness I recall,
As on an open parasol
The old pine needles fall.
SHOGETSU

The summer shower is o'er,
And midges hum above the grass
That grows upon the moor.
CHOKA

Would that my soul could drink
The dew upon the lotus flower
Here at the water's brink.
TAIGI

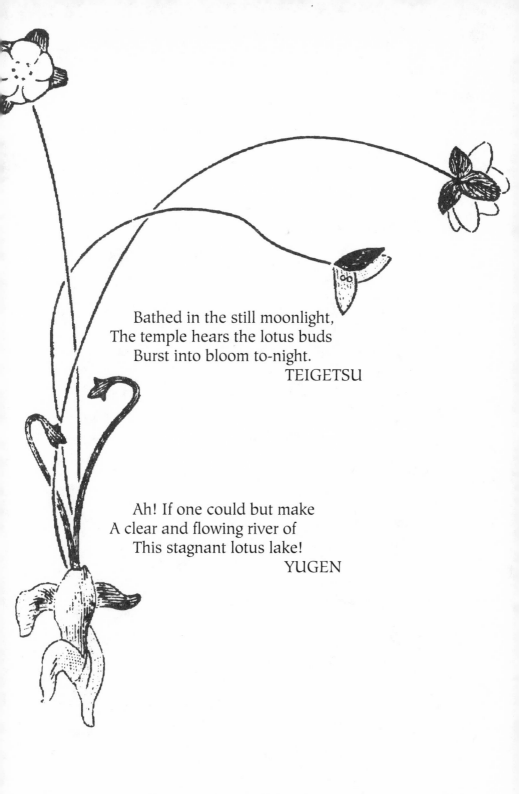

Bathed in the still moonlight,
The temple hears the lotus buds
Burst into bloom to-night.
TEIGETSU

Ah! If one could but make
A clear and flowing river of
This stagnant lotus lake!
YUGEN

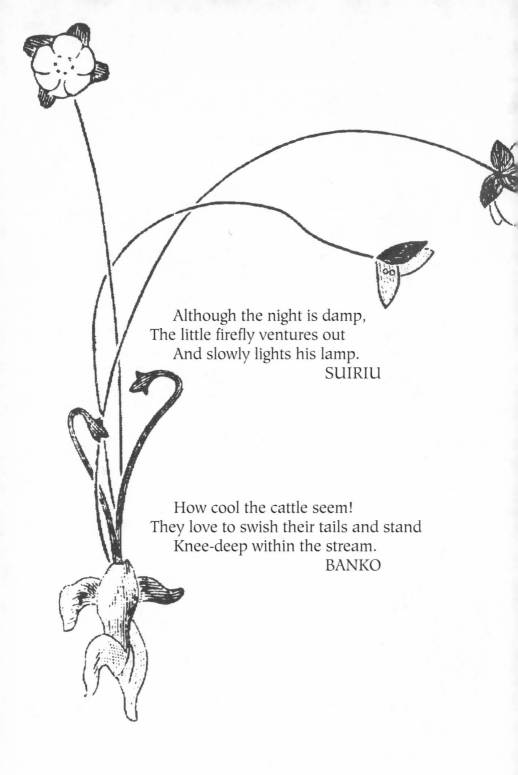

Although the night is damp,
The little firefly ventures out
And slowly lights his lamp.
SUIRIU

How cool the cattle seem!
They love to swish their tails and stand
Knee-deep within the stream.
BANKO

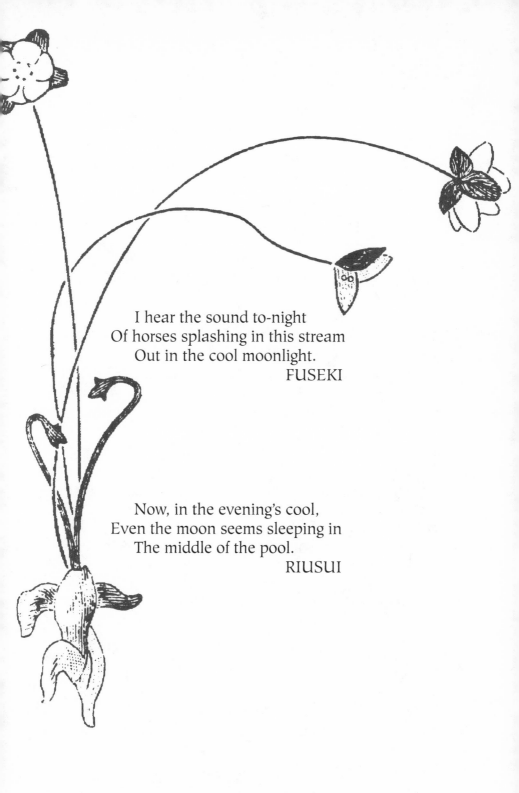

I hear the sound to-night
Of horses splashing in this stream
Out in the cool moonlight.
　　　　　FUSEKI

Now, in the evening's cool,
Even the moon seems sleeping in
The middle of the pool.
　　　　　RIUSUI

The heat is so extreme,
My heart, what little heart I've got,
Is in the Wild Duck stream.
                    SOHAKU

Under these blazing skies
The sun adds to the brilliance of
The gay-winged butterflies.
                    TAIGI

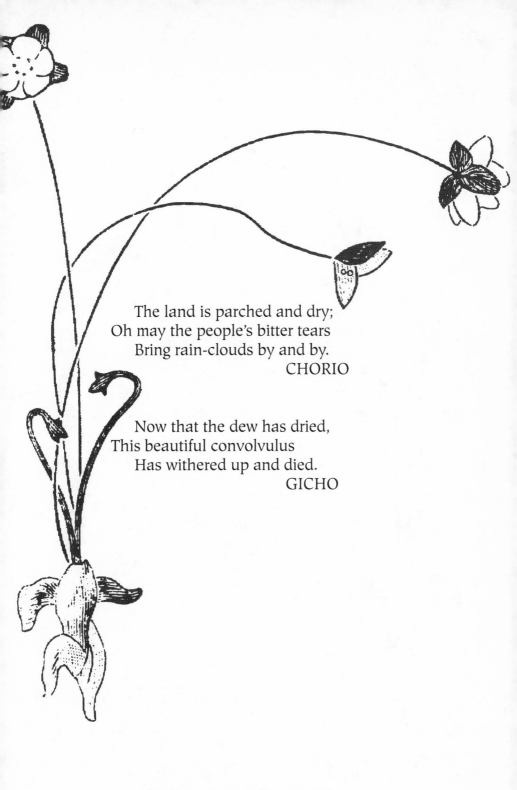

The land is parched and dry;
Oh may the people's bitter tears
Bring rain-clouds by and by.
CHORIO

Now that the dew has dried,
This beautiful convolvulus
Has withered up and died.
GICHO

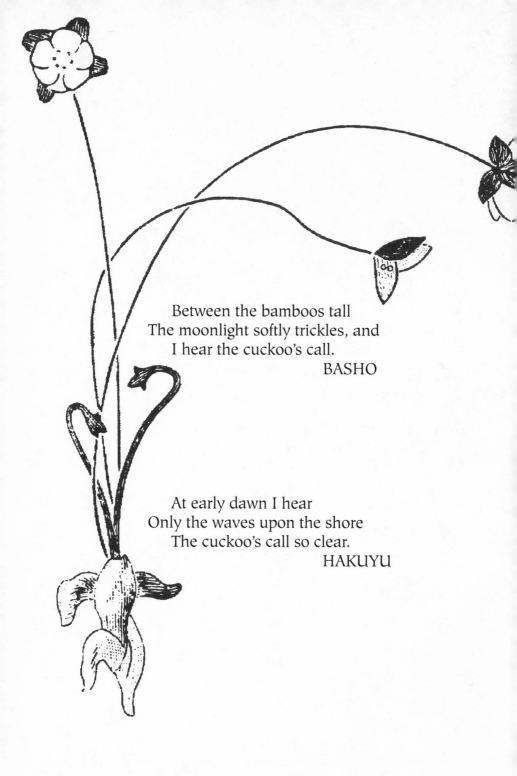

Between the bamboos tall
The moonlight softly trickles, and
I hear the cuckoo's call.
                    BASHO

At early dawn I hear
Only the waves upon the shore
The cuckoo's call so clear.
                    HAKUYU

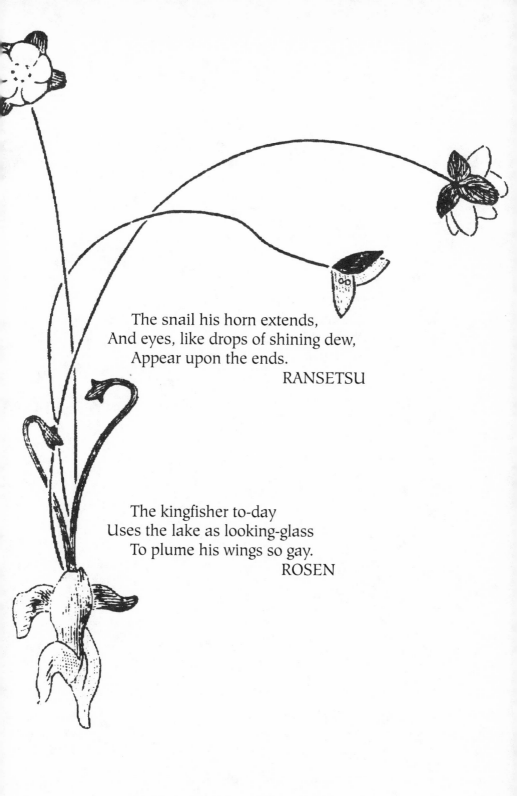

The snail his horn extends,
And eyes, like drops of shining dew,
Appear upon the ends.
RANSETSU

The kingfisher to-day
Uses the lake as looking-glass
To plume his wings so gay.
ROSEN

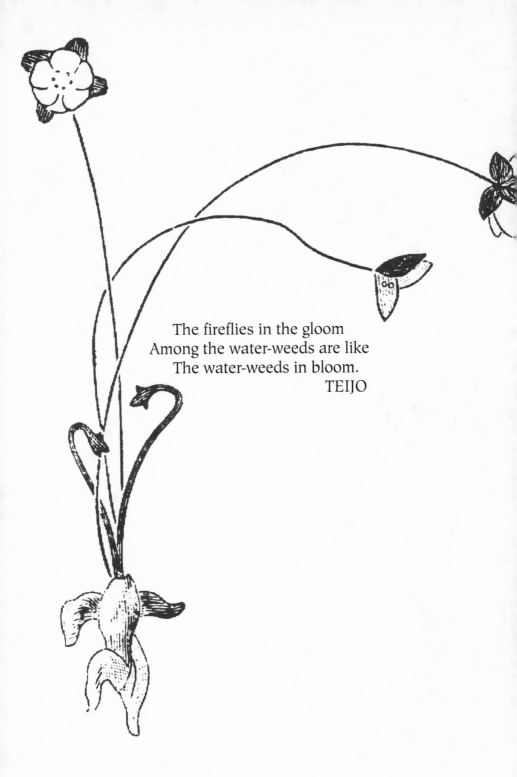

The fireflies in the gloom
Among the water-weeds are like
The water-weeds in bloom.
TEIJO

AUTUMN

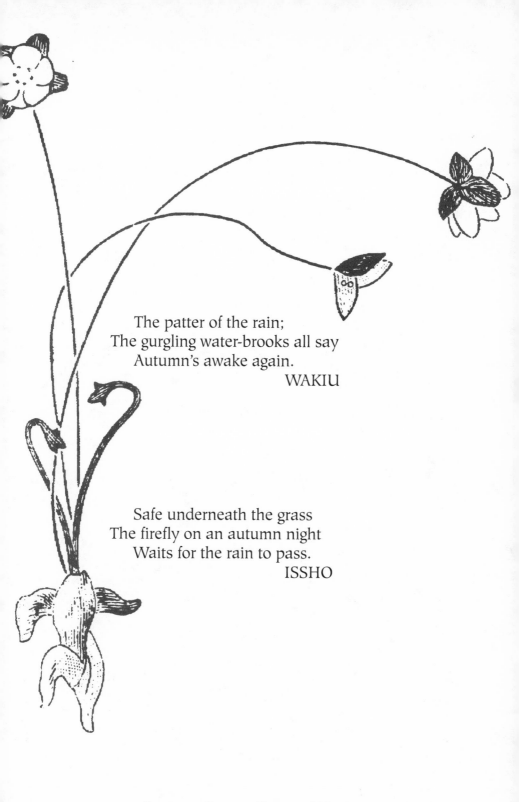

The patter of the rain;
The gurgling water-brooks all say
Autumn's awake again.
WAKIU

Safe underneath the grass
The firefly on an autumn night
Waits for the rain to pass.
ISSHO

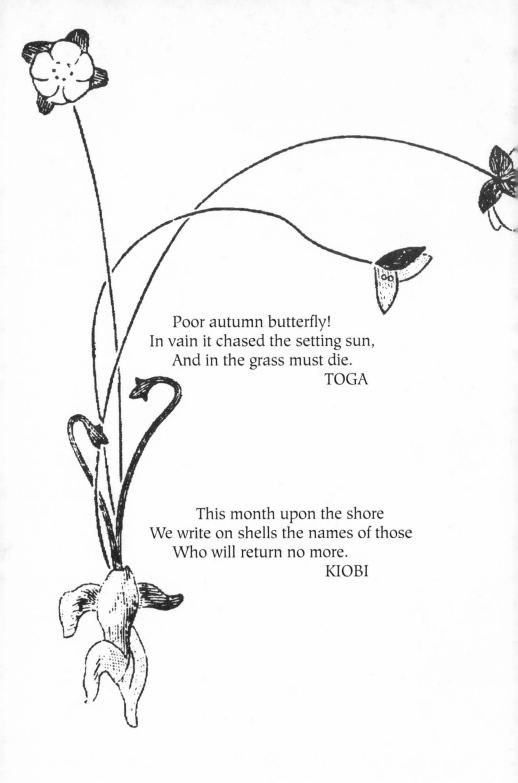

Poor autumn butterfly!
In vain it chased the setting sun,
And in the grass must die.
TOGA

This month upon the shore
We write on shells the names of those
Who will return no more.
KIOBI

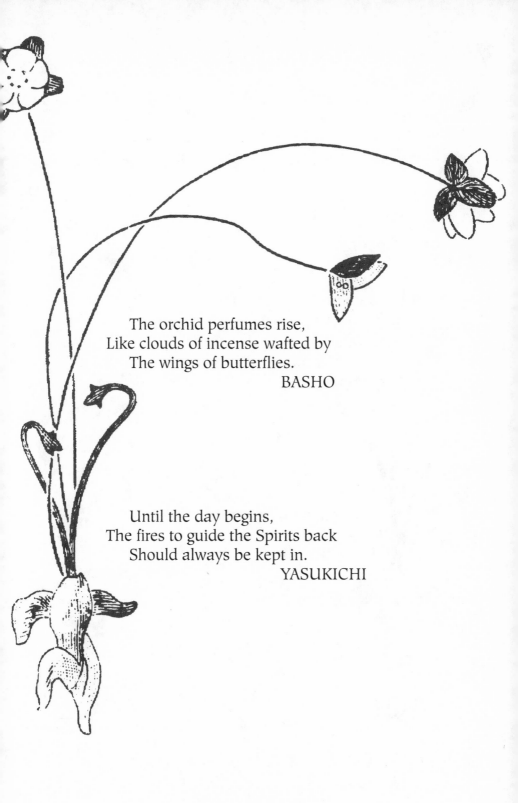

The orchid perfumes rise,
Like clouds of incense wafted by
The wings of butterflies.
BASHO

Until the day begins,
The fires to guide the Spirits back
Should always be kept in.
YASUKICHI

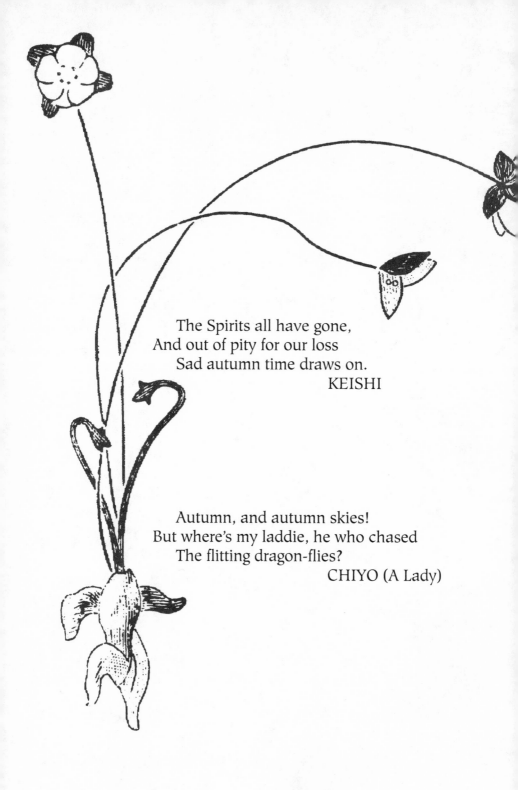

The Spirits all have gone,
And out of pity for our loss
Sad autumn time draws on.
KEISHI

Autumn, and autumn skies!
But where's my laddie, he who chased
The flitting dragon-flies?
CHIYO (A Lady)

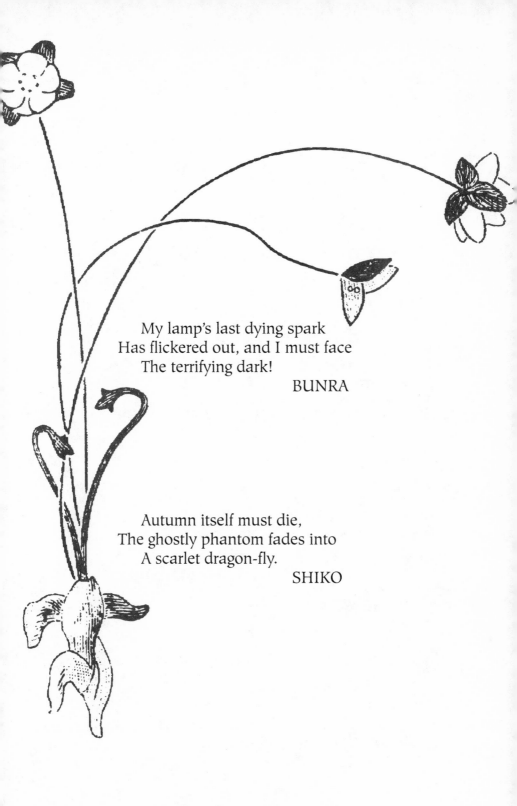

My lamp's last dying spark
Has flickered out, and I must face
The terrifying dark!
                    BUNRA

Autumn itself must die,
The ghostly phantom fades into
A scarlet dragon-fly.
                    SHIKO

September's here again,
And thickly lies the morning dew
Upon both hill and plain.
                    RIUN

The breeze across the plain
Has waved the wild bush clover, but
The dewdrops still remain.
                    BASHO

The lotus is in flower,
And very trying to the bees
Must be the sunset hour.
                    KIOTAI

This life we leave behind
Is like the shadow of a dance
Seen on a window-blind.
                    GENSUI

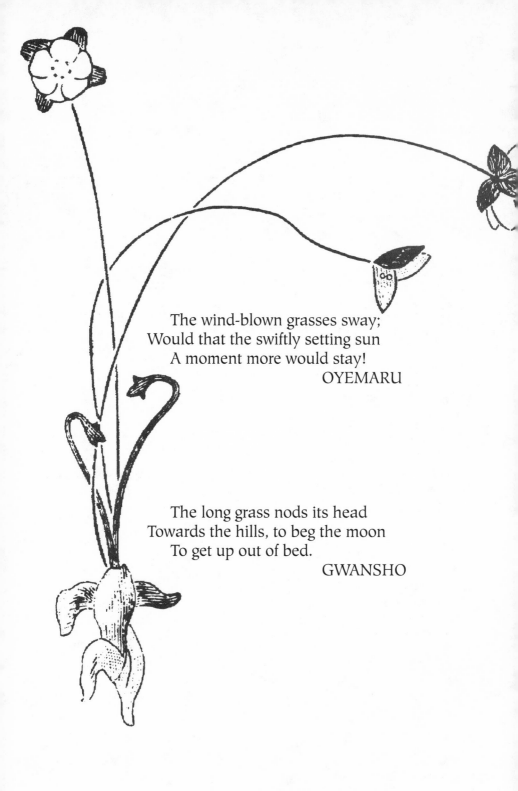

The wind-blown grasses sway;
Would that the swiftly setting sun
A moment more would stay!

OYEMARU

The long grass nods its head
Towards the hills, to beg the moon
To get up out of bed.

GWANSHO

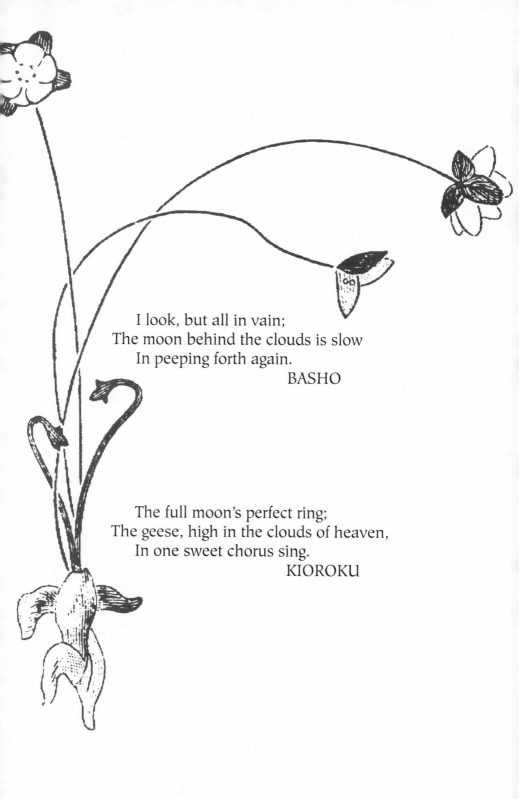

I look, but all in vain;
The moon behind the clouds is slow
In peeping forth again.
BASHO

The full moon's perfect ring;
The geese, high in the clouds of heaven,
In one sweet chorus sing.
KIOROKU

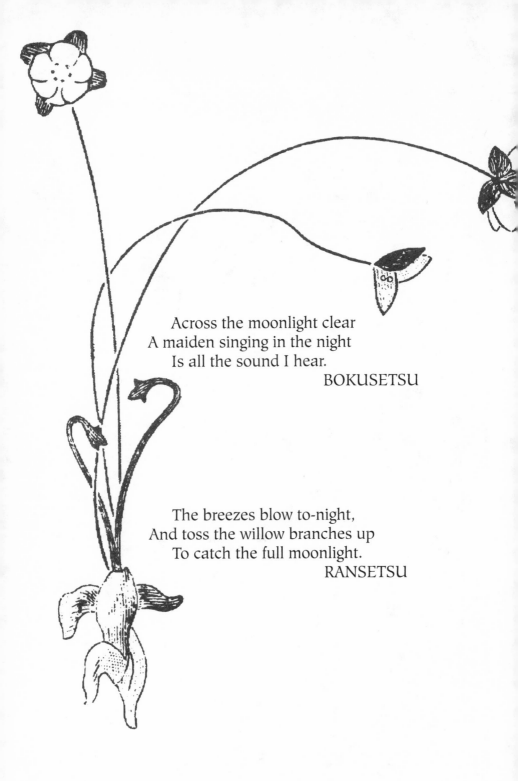

Across the moonlight clear
A maiden singing in the night
Is all the sound I hear.
                    BOKUSETSU

The breezes blow to-night,
And toss the willow branches up
To catch the full moonlight.
                    RANSETSU

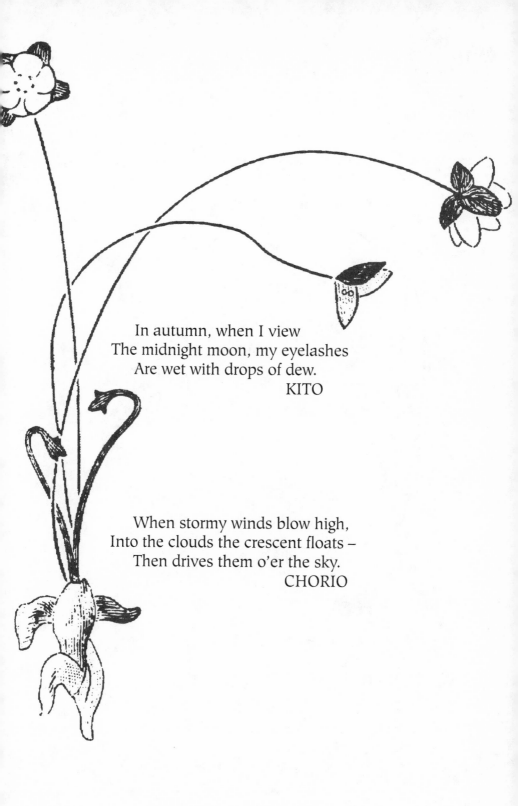

In autumn, when I view
The midnight moon, my eyelashes
Are wet with drops of dew.
                    KITO

When stormy winds blow high,
Into the clouds the crescent floats –
Then drives them o'er the sky.
                    CHORIO

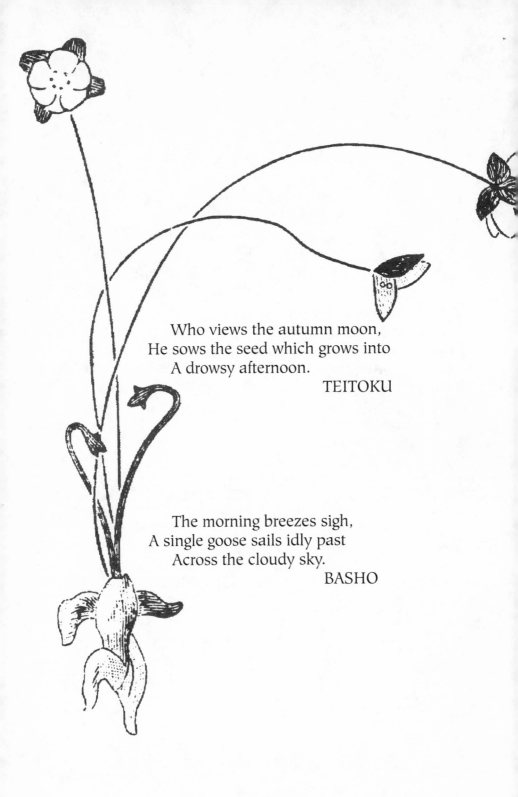

Who views the autumn moon,
He sows the seed which grows into
A drowsy afternoon.

TEITOKU

The morning breezes sigh,
A single goose sails idly past
Across the cloudy sky.

BASHO

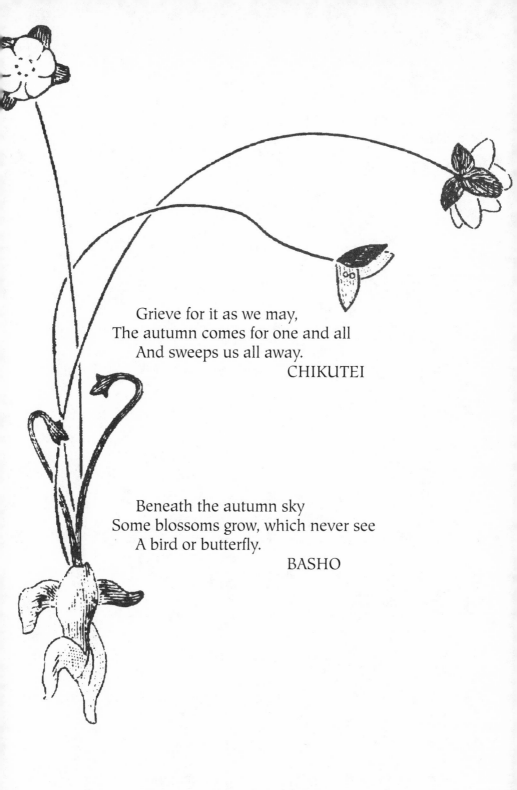

Grieve for it as we may,
The autumn comes for one and all
And sweeps us all away.
                    CHIKUTEI

Beneath the autumn sky
Some blossoms grow, which never see
A bird or butterfly.
                    BASHO

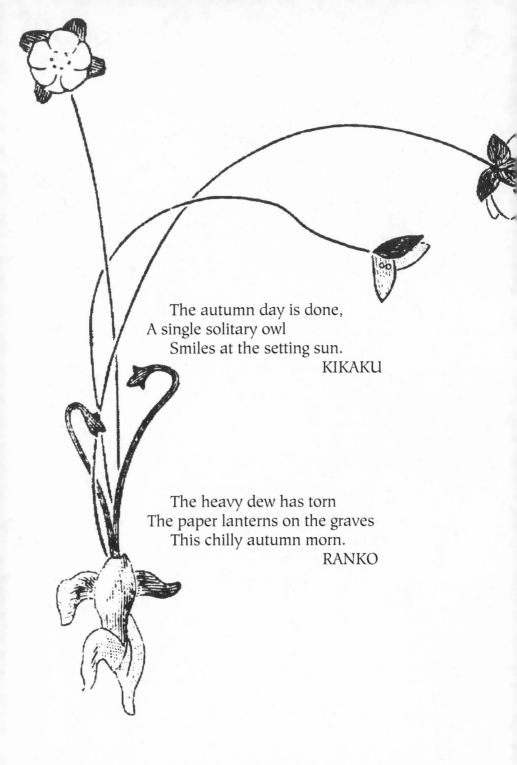

The autumn day is done,
A single solitary owl
Smiles at the setting sun.
                    KIKAKU

The heavy dew has torn
The paper lanterns on the graves
This chilly autumn morn.
                    RANKO

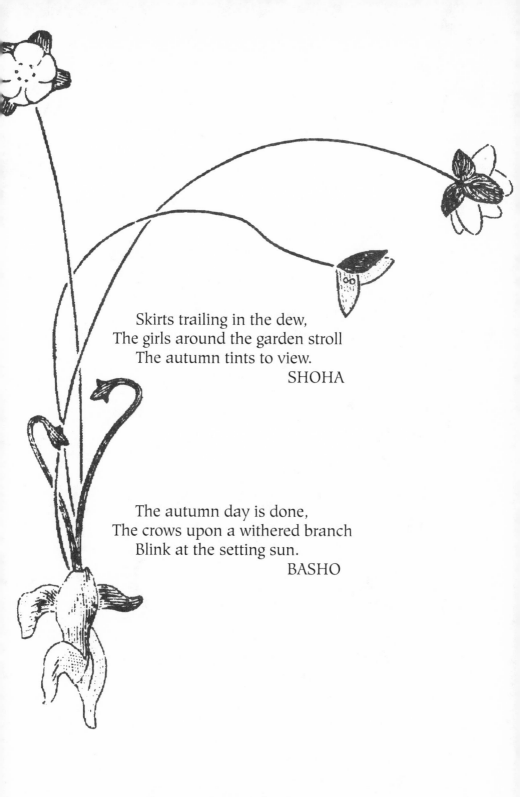

Skirts trailing in the dew,
The girls around the garden stroll
The autumn tints to view.
SHOHA

The autumn day is done,
The crows upon a withered branch
Blink at the setting sun.
BASHO

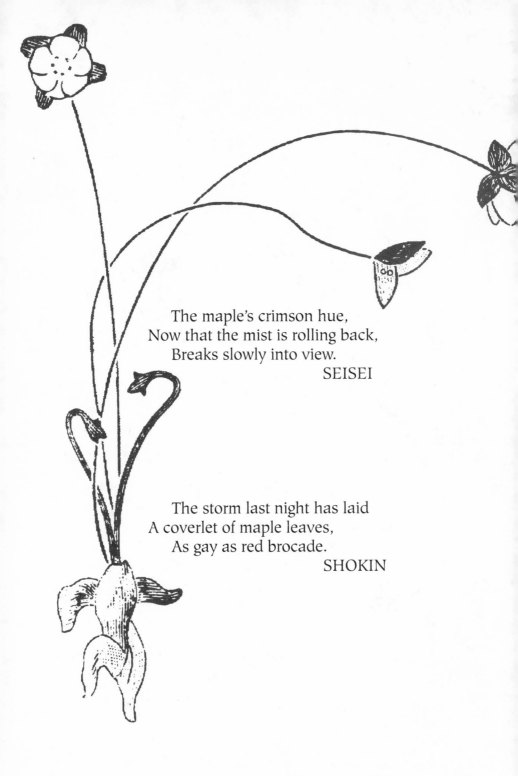

The maple's crimson hue,
Now that the mist is rolling back,
Breaks slowly into view.

SEISEI

The storm last night has laid
A coverlet of maple leaves,
As gay as red brocade.

SHOKIN

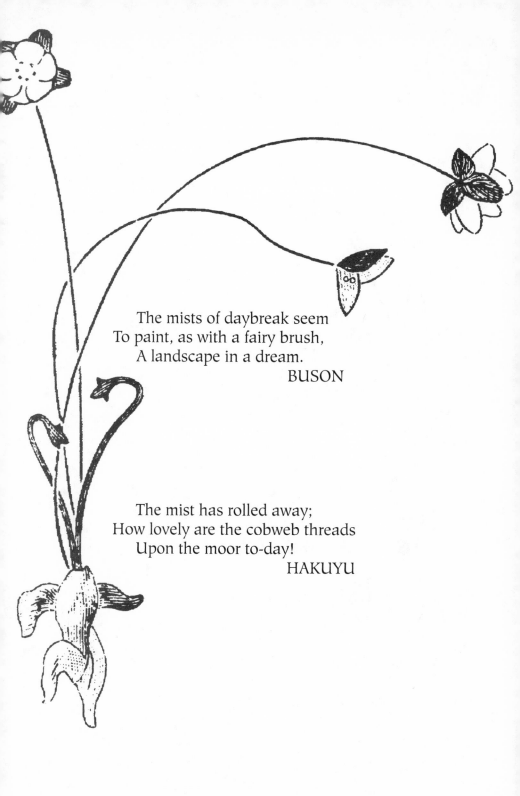

The mists of daybreak seem
To paint, as with a fairy brush,
A landscape in a dream.
BUSON

The mist has rolled away;
How lovely are the cobweb threads
Upon the moor to-day!
HAKUYU

The lightning-flash so bright
Serves only to intensify
The blackness of the night.
                    SEKIRAN

The ivy's stripped and bare;
No longer can the autumn wind
Blow softly rustling there.
                    KAKIU

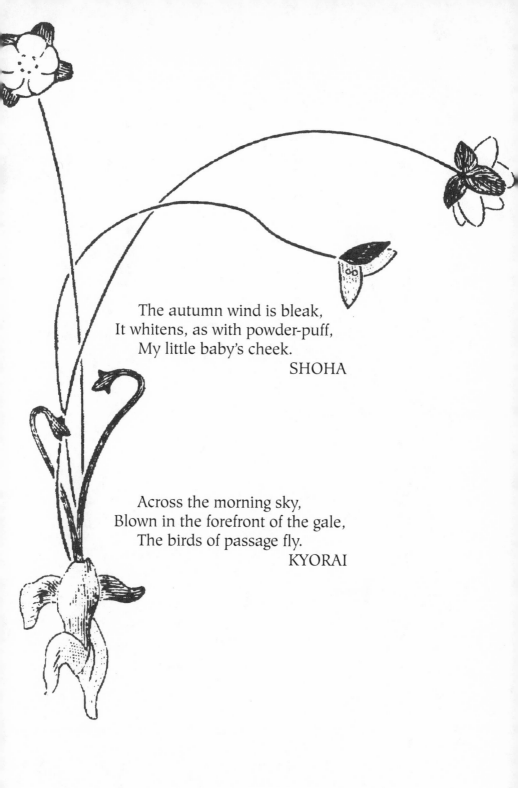

The autumn wind is bleak,
It whitens, as with powder-puff,
My little baby's cheek.
SHOHA

Across the morning sky,
Blown in the forefront of the gale,
The birds of passage fly.
KYORAI

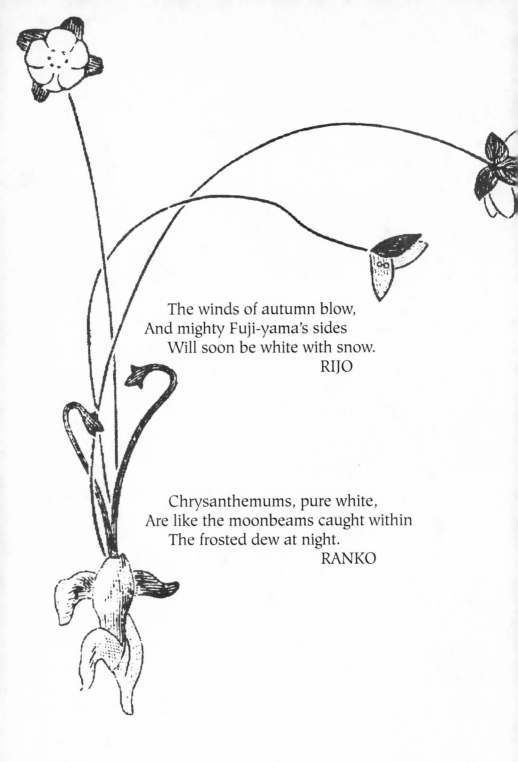

The winds of autumn blow,
And mighty Fuji-yama's sides
Will soon be white with snow.
                    RIJO

Chrysanthemums, pure white,
Are like the moonbeams caught within
The frosted dew at night.
                    RANKO

I dwell here all alone,
For no one passes by this road
Now that the autumn's gone.
                    BASHO

Autumn is well nigh past,
And maple-trees upon the road
Their crimson leaves have cast.
                    OTSUYU

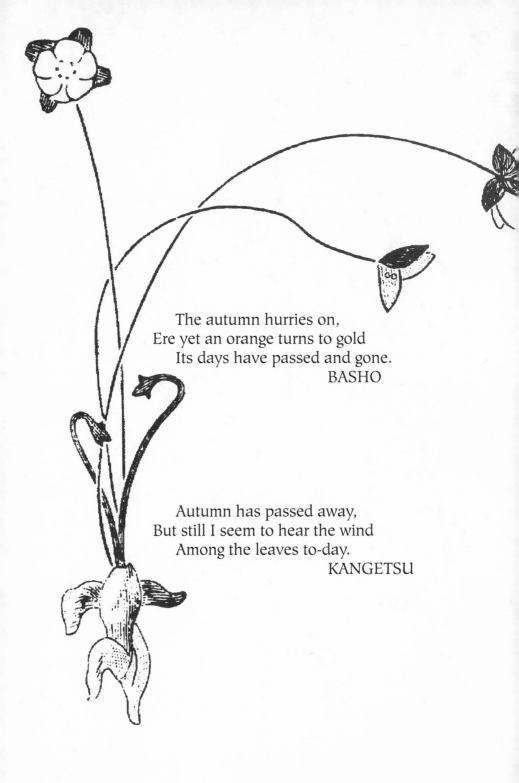

The autumn hurries on,
Ere yet an orange turns to gold
Its days have passed and gone.
BASHO

Autumn has passed away,
But still I seem to hear the wind
Among the leaves to-day.
KANGETSU

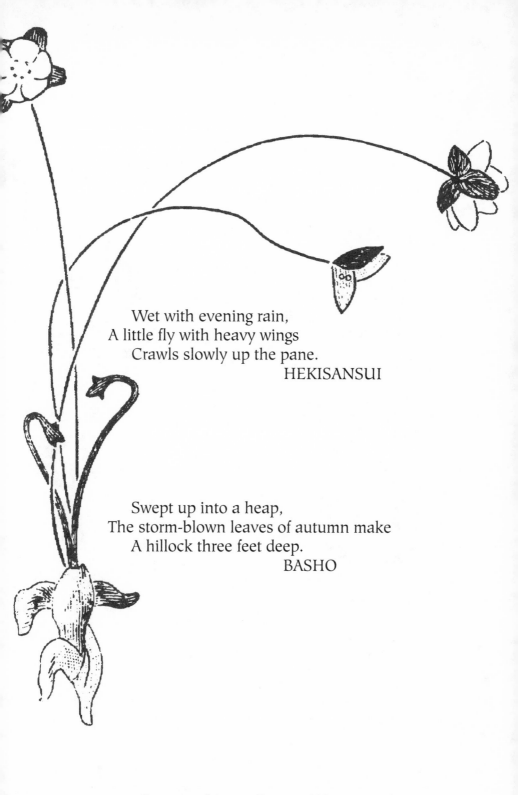

Wet with evening rain,
A little fly with heavy wings
Crawls slowly up the pane.
HEKISANSUI

Swept up into a heap,
The storm-blown leaves of autumn make
A hillock three feet deep.
BASHO

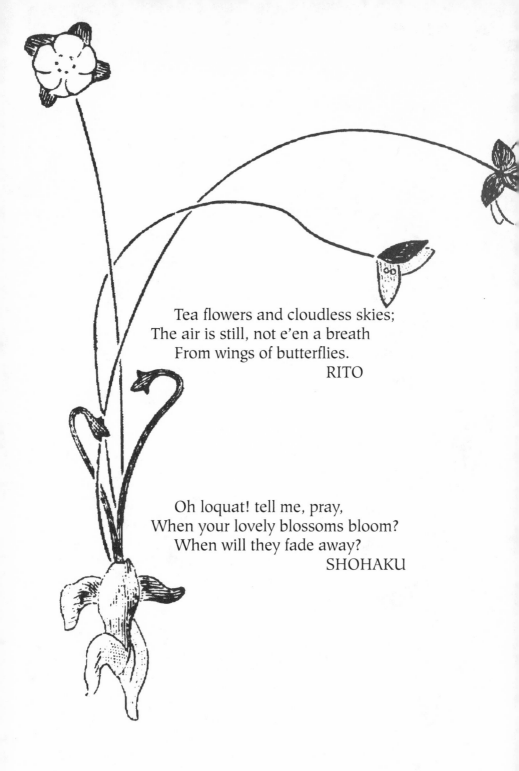

Tea flowers and cloudless skies;
The air is still, not e'en a breath
From wings of butterflies.
                              RITO

Oh loquat! tell me, pray,
When your lovely blossoms bloom?
When will they fade away?
                              SHOHAKU

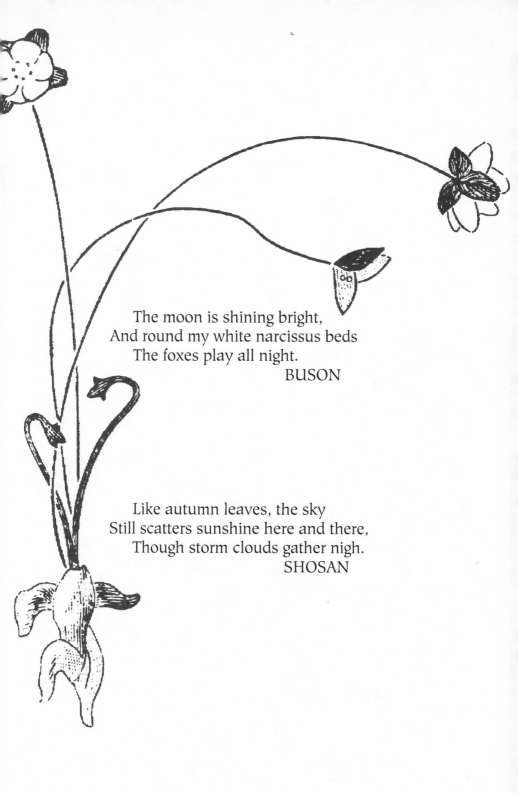

The moon is shining bright,
And round my white narcissus beds
The foxes play all night.
                    BUSON

Like autumn leaves, the sky
Still scatters sunshine here and there,
Though storm clouds gather nigh.
                    SHOSAN

A fallen leaf is dead!
But after death the leaves have got
No gates of Hell to dread.
SOKAN

With harsh and rustling sound
The dead leaves fall – the petals drop
In silence to the ground.
MORITAKE

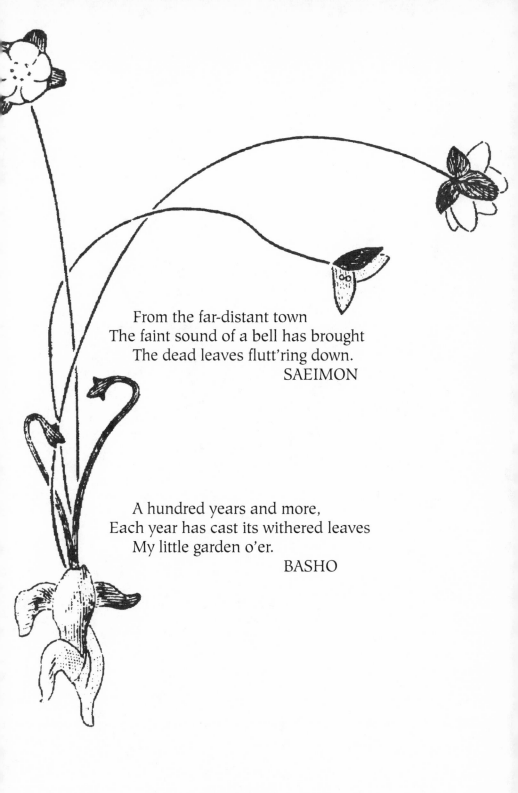

From the far-distant town
The faint sound of a bell has brought
The dead leaves flutt'ring down.
                    SAEIMON

A hundred years and more,
Each year has cast its withered leaves
My little garden o'er.
                    BASHO

ODES

Landscapes of Life and Love

The pleasant spring hath passed away,
   Now summer follows close, I ween,
And Ama's secret summit may
   In all its grandeur now be seen;
     Of yore the drying ground,
Whitened with angels' robes, spread far
  around.

       JI-TO TEN-WO

Now 'mid the hills the Momiji
　　Is trampled down 'neath hoof of dear,
Whose plaintive cries continually
　　Are heard both far and near;
　　　My shivering frame
Now autumn's piercing chills doth blame.
　　　　SARU-MARU TA-IU

Thy love hath passed away from me
　Left desolate, forlorn –
In winter-rains how wearily
　The summer past I mourn!
　　　　　ONONO-KO-MACHI

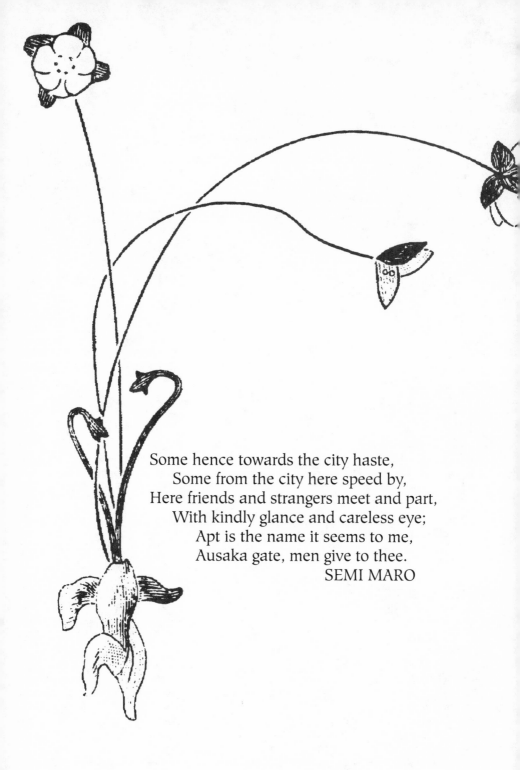

Some hence towards the city haste,
Some from the city here speed by,
Here friends and strangers meet and part,
With kindly glance and careless eye;
Apt is the name it seems to me,
Ausaka gate, men give to thee.
SEMI MARO

Thy wishes, love, I have obeyed,
And 'mid the meadows have I strayed
In this spring-time, and sought with care
The wakana plant that groweth there.
    Lo on my sleeve
The falling snow its trace doth leave.
KWO-KO TEN-WO

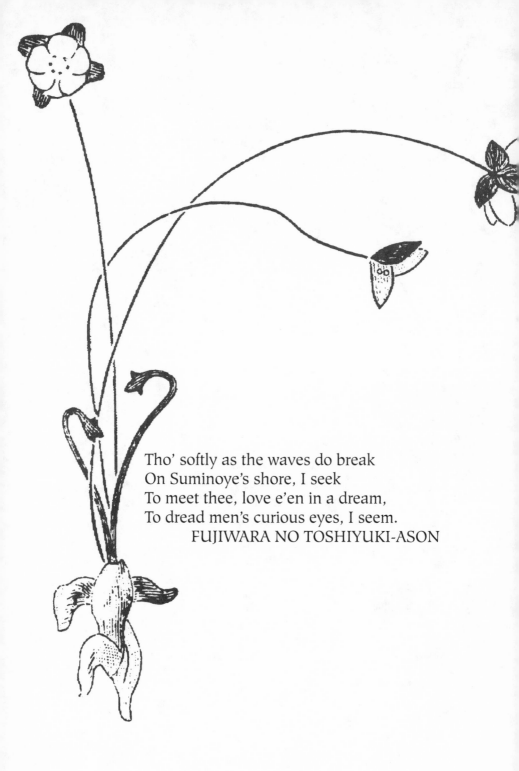

Tho' softly as the waves do break
On Suminoye's shore, I seek
To meet thee, love e'en in a dream,
To dread men's curious eyes, I seem.
                    FUJIWARA NO TOSHIYUKI-ASON

Distracted by my misery.
How utterly forlorn am I;
Oh that I might thee once more see,
Tho' it should cost my life to me!

MOTOYOSHI SHIN-WO

Oh maiden! heedless of thy vow,
    Why com'st thou not? 'Tis "long-moon"
    night,
And th' Ariake moon shines now,
    Forgetfullness with welcome light.
                    SOSEI HOSHI

Now autumn's gales, in various freak,
On herb, on tree, destruction wreak,
　　　And wildest roar
The gusts that down from Mube pour.
　　　　　BUNYA NO YASUHIDE

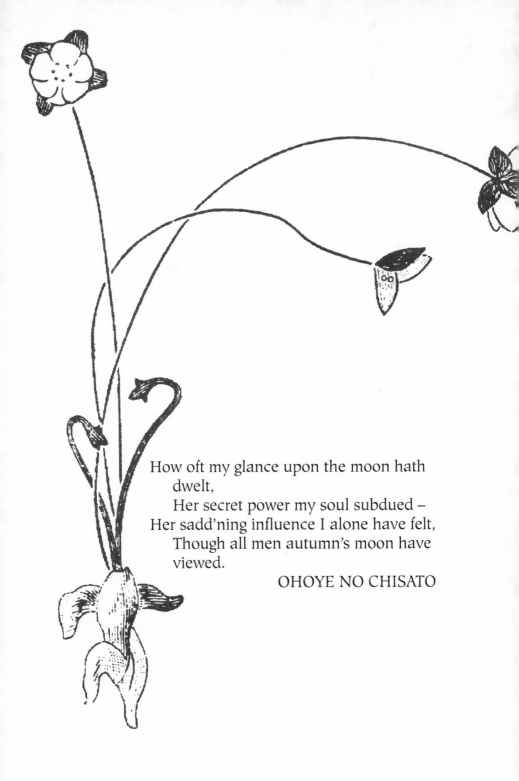

How oft my glance upon the moon hath dwelt,
Her secret power my soul subdued –
Her sadd'ning influence I alone have felt,
Though all men autumn's moon have viewed.

OHOYE NO CHISATO

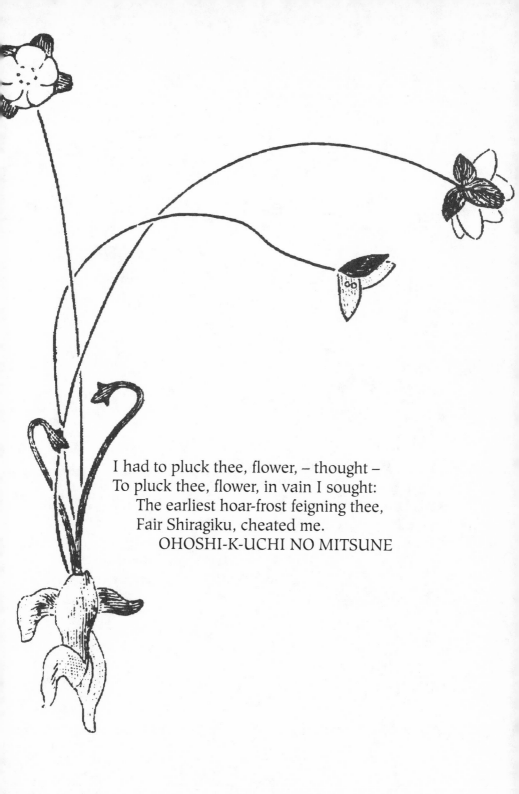

I had to pluck thee, flower, – thought –
To pluck thee, flower, in vain I sought:
    The earliest hoar-frost feigning thee,
    Fair Shiragiku, cheated me.
        OHOSHI-K-UCHI NO MITSUNE

The winds of autumn have amassed
    Dried withered leaves in ruddy heaps,
Have them in th' mountain-torrent cast,
    Whose stream in stony channel sweeps;
    Amid the rocks that bar the way
    The Mom-ji's reddened leaves delay.
    HARU-MICHI NO TSURAKI

'Tis a pleasant day of merry spring,
No bitter frosts are threatening,
No storm-winds blow, no rain-clouds low'r,
    The sun shines bright on high,
Yet thou, poor trembling little flow'r,
    Dost wither away and die.
                    KINO TOMO-NORI

Of old companions bereft,
   Men's friendship more I may not seek,
Nought but the ancient pine-trees left,
   That grown on Takasago's peak,
    Comrades of many a year now gone,
    But not the friends for whom I mourn.
      FUJIWARA NO OKIKAZE

The comrades of my early days
   Their former friend indifferent view,
Who with a wandering eye doth gaze
   On th' village that of old he knew
     So well. O flower! Thy fragrancy
     Alone familiar seems to me.
             KI NO TSURAYUKI

'Twas a summer's night, I scarcely thought
    The evening hours had passed away
When dawn broke; long the moon I'd
    sought,
    Now knew where 'mid the clouds she lay.
    KYOWARA NO FUKAYABA

Now dew-drops sparkling o'er the moor are
    seen,
  The autumn gusts sweeps howling by,
Scarce lurks an instant 'mid the reeds
    I ween:
      In timid show'r the dew-drops fly,
      And, scattered o'er the grass, there lie.
        BUNYA NO ASAYASU

Tho' aye I strive my lot to hide,
  My face to all the secret tells:
My changing visage, sorely tried,
  Shows that deep passion in me dwells:
    And all men ask,
What griefs my altered features task?
          TAIRA NO KANEMORI

I went to meet thee, dearest maid,
   And when I parted loth from thee,
Upon my soul such mis'ry weighed,
   I mourned the love that burdened me:
     O that my heart
Were still unvexed by lovers smart!
     CHIU-NAGON ATSUTADA

To love, were it not human fate,
    Then men their fellows would not shun,
Their very selves they would not hate,
    As since love's birth they've ever done.
            CHIU-NAGON ASATADA

Ah, cruel one! Thou pass'dst me by,
   No glance of pity on me turned,
A careless scorn was in thine eye,
   That mock'd the passion that in me
   burn'd:
     Alas! Alas!
Such woes my falling pow'rs surpass.
      KEN-TOKU KO

The fishers' barques in safety glide
    O'er th' broad expanse of Yura's bay,
Their rudder lost o'er Yura's tide,
    In vague uncertain path they stray:
    The course of love doth, too,
    A like uncertain path pursue.
        SONE NO YOSHITADA

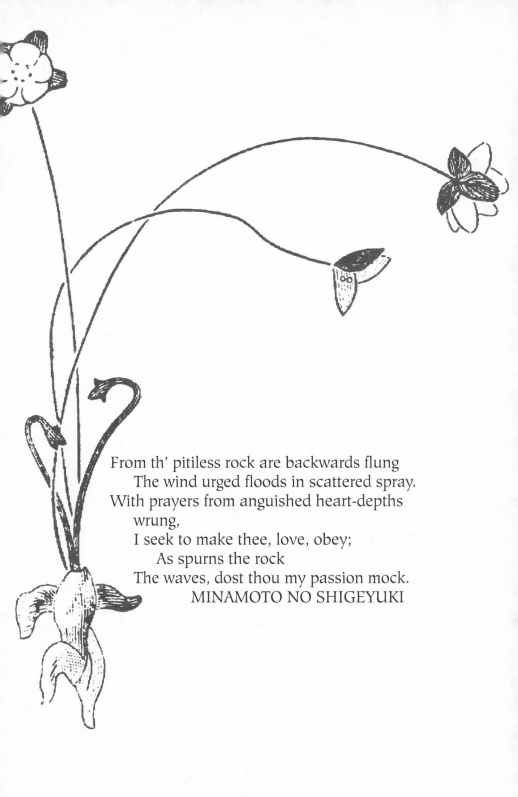

From th' pitiless rock are backwards flung
   The wind urged floods in scattered spray.
With prayers from anguished heart-depths
   wrung,
   I seek to make thee, love, obey;
     As spurns the rock
The waves, dost thou my passion mock.
    MINAMOTO NO SHIGEYUKI

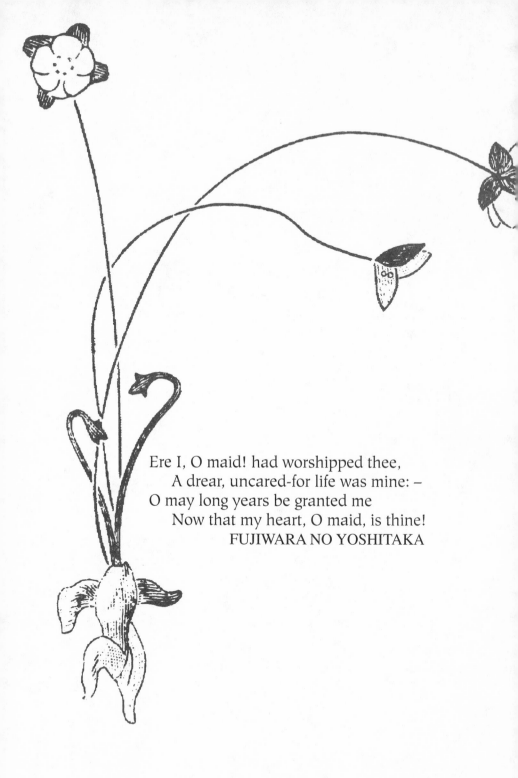

Ere I, O maid! had worshipped thee,
    A drear, uncared-for life was mine: –
O may long years be granted me
    Now that my heart, O maid, is thine!
    FUJIWARA NO YOSHITAKA

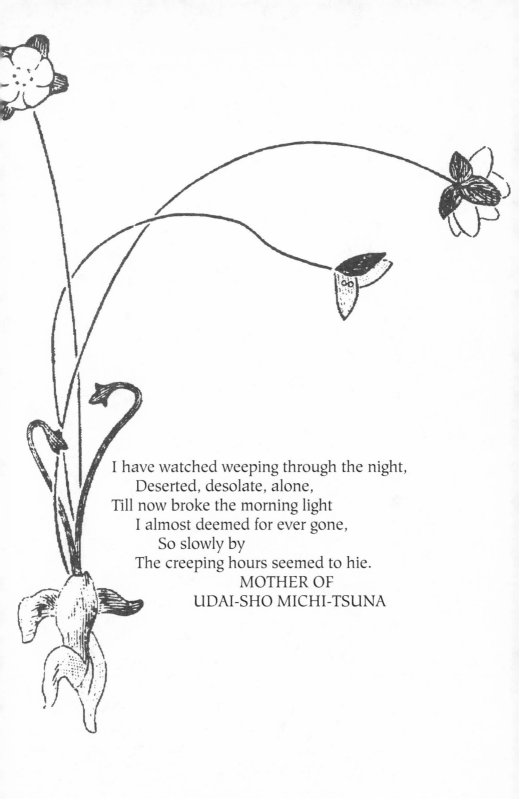

I have watched weeping through the night,
   Deserted, desolate, alone,
Till now broke the morning light
   I almost deemed for ever gone,
     So slowly by
The creeping hours seemed to hie.
      MOTHER OF
   UDAI-SHO MICHI-TSUNA

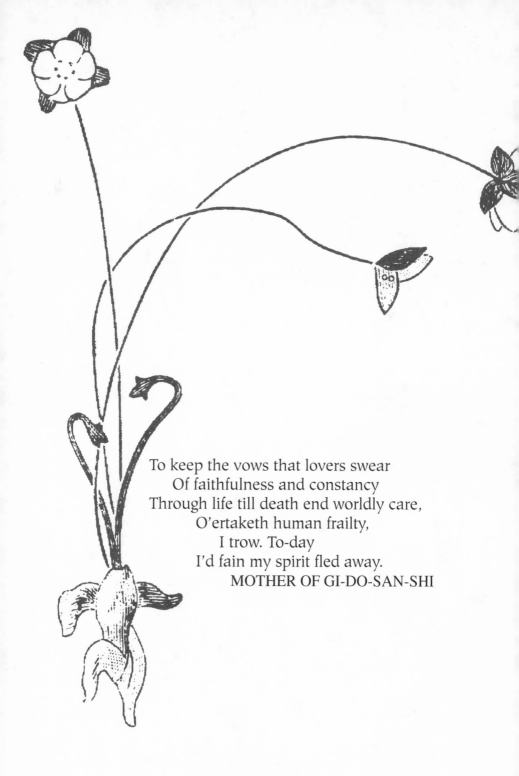

To keep the vows that lovers swear
Of faithfulness and constancy
Through life till death end worldly care,
O'ertaketh human frailty,
I trow. To-day
I'd fain my spirit fled away.
MOTHER OF GI-DO-SAN-SHI

To tell thee of my love were vain,
    Its depth to me is scarcely known:
As writhes the flesh 'neath Moxa's pain,
    The Moxa on Ibuki grown,
      So madly writhes my spirit 'mong
Love's flames, ere now unknown, sore wrung.
    FUJIWARA NO SANE-KATA-ASON

When day breaks, tho' full well I know
   The darkness of the ensuing night
The hated day shall overthrow:
   Yet aye the daylight do I hate,
     And bitterly mourn
   Th' unwelcome breaking of the dawn.
     FUJIWARA NO MICHINOBU-ASON

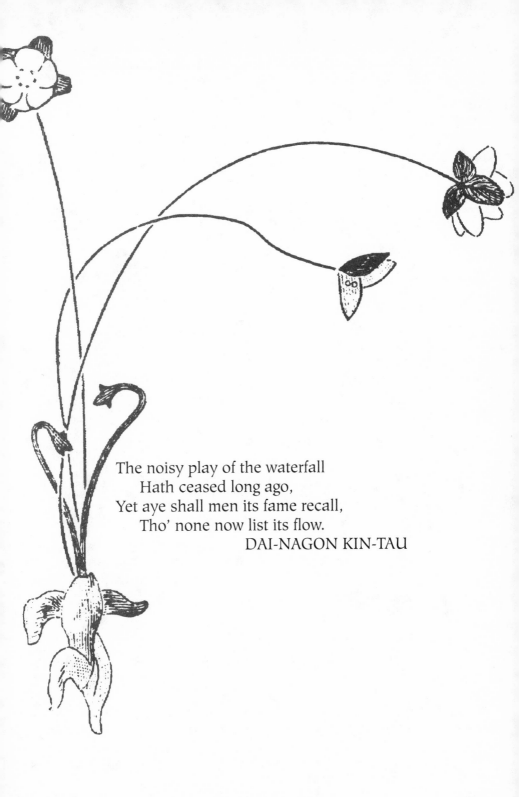

The noisy play of the waterfall
   Hath ceased long ago,
Yet aye shall men its fame recall,
  Tho' none now list its flow.
        DAI-NAGON KIN-TAU

Ere long for me this world shall end,
　Thus doth my mind to me foretell;
Ere long to other world shall wend
　My soul that thee hath lov'd so well.
　　Ah! would that thou
　But once more wer't beside me now.
　　　　　IDS'MI SH'KIBU

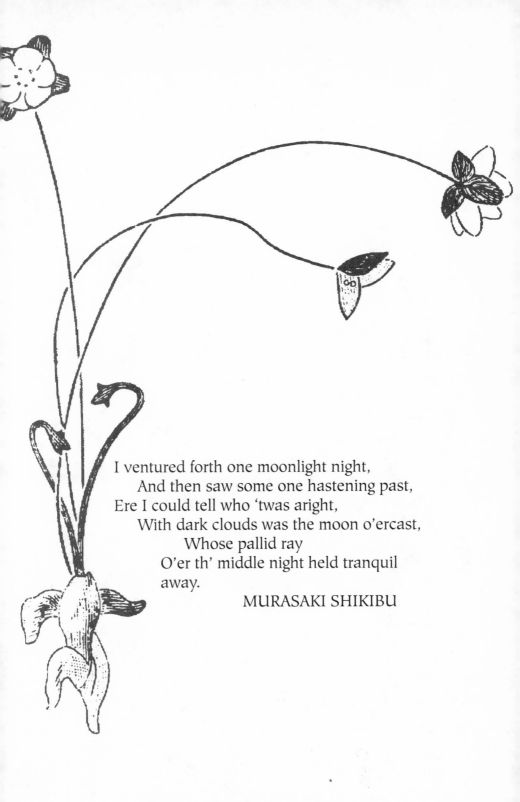

I ventured forth one moonlight night,
   And then saw some one hastening past,
Ere I could tell who 'twas aright,
   With dark clouds was the moon o'ercast,
     Whose pallid ray
   O'er th' middle night held tranquil
away.

     MURASAKI SHIKIBU

More fickle thou then th' winds that pour
Down Arima o'er Ina's moor,
And still my love for thee as yet
I have forgotten to forget.
                    DAI-NI NO SAMMI

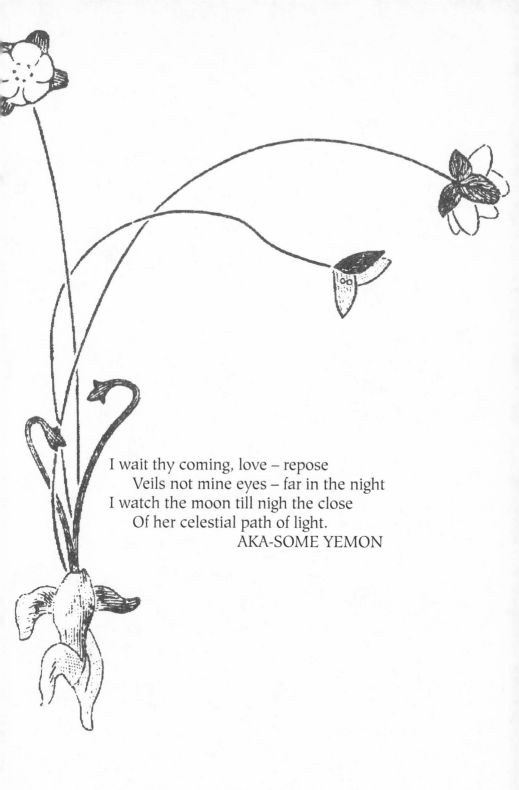

I wait thy coming, love – repose
    Veils not mine eyes – far in the night
I watch the moon till nigh the close
    Of her celestial path of light.
               AKA-SOME YEMON

Now doth deep misery oppress
My vex'd and sorrow'd mind
To none will I my woe confess,
Save thee, among mankind:
With thee I seek
Of all my wretchedness to speak.
SAKYO NO TAIFU MICHIMASA

By th' dim grey light of early dawn
   I stray'd by Uji's wave,
From whence the rifting mist upborne
   Me scattered glimpses gave
      Of Zeke's stakes there set,
   Whereon the fisher spreads his net.
      GON-CHIU-NAGON TADAYORI

Despised, I weep thy long neglect,
My tears drench my sleeve,
The happiness of my life is wrecked
In struggles to achieve
Thy stubborn love:
My fate might all men's pity move.
SAGAMI

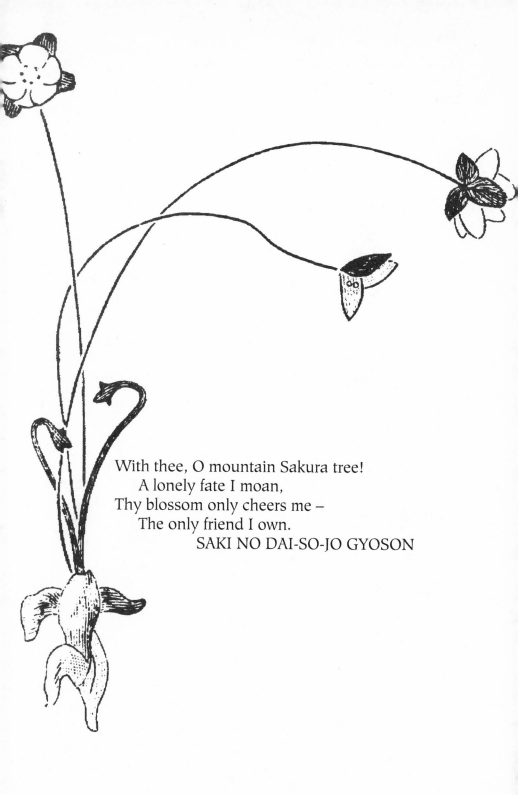

With thee, O mountain Sakura tree!
 A lonely fate I moan,
Thy blossom only cheers me –
 The only friend I own.
          SAKI NO DAI-SO-JO GYOSON

Had I made of thy proffer'd arm
  A pillow for my wearied head,
No longer e'en than lasts the charm
  Of a spring-night's dream – what had
  rumour said?
      How would my fame
      Have suffer'd from men's sland'ring
  blame!

SUWO NO NAISHI

Fain would I in this world so hard
    No longer live, but still must stay: –
How wistfully my eyes regard
    The midnight moonbeams' tranquil sway!
    SANJO NO IN

In lonely solitude my home,
    And from my cabin when I stray,
Where'er my wand'ring eyes may roam,
    The landscape that doth round me lay,
        How desolate, how drear
        Doth it at autumn-e'en appear.
            RYOZEN HOSHI

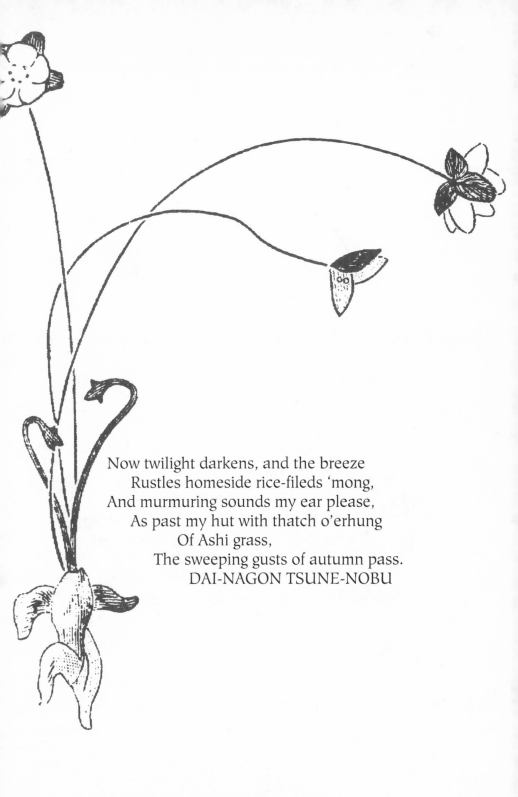

Now twilight darkens, and the breeze
   Rustles homeside rice-fileds 'mong,
And murmuring sounds my ear please,
   As past my hut with thatch o'erhung
     Of Ashi grass,
   The sweeping gusts of autumn pass.
      DAI-NAGON TSUNE-NOBU

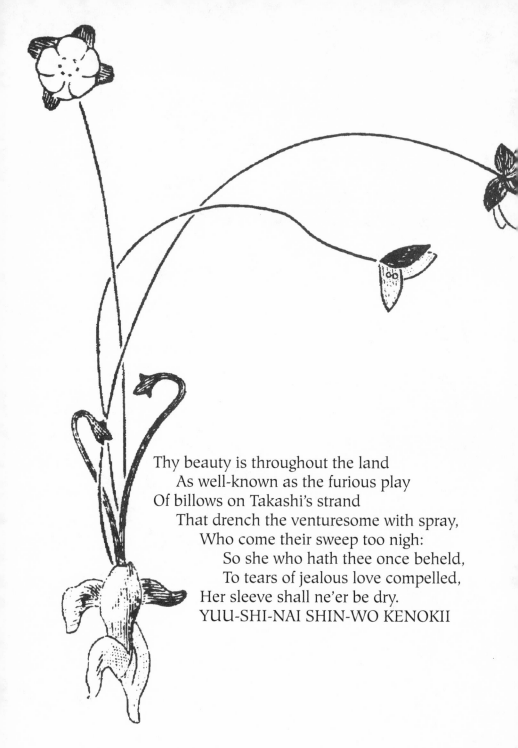

Thy beauty is throughout the land
   As well-known as the furious play
Of billows on Takashi's strand
   That drench the venturesome with spray,
    Who come their sweep too nigh:
     So she who hath thee once beheld,
     To tears of jealous love compelled,
Her sleeve shall ne'er be dry.
YUU-SHI-NAI SHIN-WO KENOKII

A covenant thou mad'st with me,
    And as the Sasemo from th' dew,
So I my very life from thee
Drink in. Alas! I fear me
    This autumn's days are now but few!
        FUJIWARA NO MOTOTOSHI

In fisher's barque I onward glide
O'er th' broad expanse of ocean's tide,
And towards th' horizon when I turn
My glance I scarcely can discern
Where the white-tipped billows end,
That with the cloud-horizon blend.

DAIJO-DAIJIN

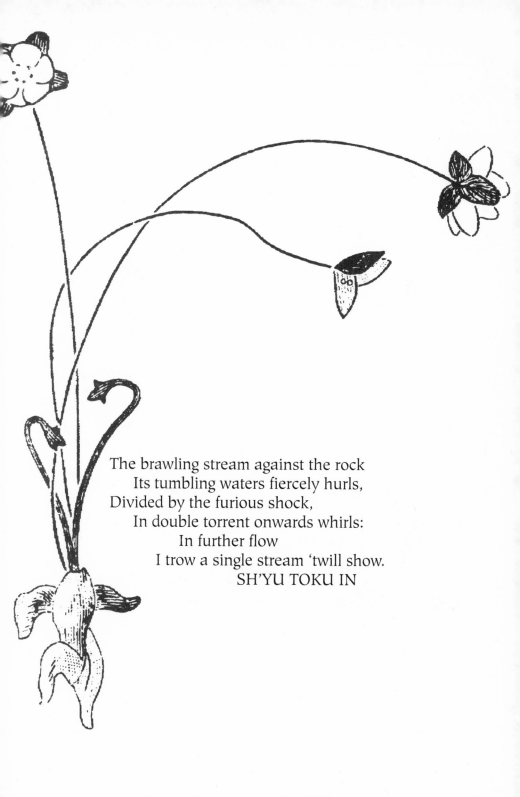

The brawling stream against the rock
 Its tumbling waters fiercely hurls,
Divided by the furious shock,
 In double torrent onwards whirls:
  In further flow
 I trow a single stream 'twill show.
   SH'YU TOKU IN

When bloweth autumn's chilly blast,
    Through rifts at times the moonbeams
        peep,
From 'mid the dark clouds drifting past,
    And earth in pallid radiance steep,
        I love to see
        The bright-edged shadows o'er the lea.
SAKYO NO TAIU AKISUKE

What wretchedness is mine, O Life!
　　With what deep mis'ry thou'rt opprest!
With my sad lot I strive in strife,
　　That leaveth me nor peace nor rest;
　　　　The tears that flow
　　Down o'er my cheek my anguish
show.

　　　　　　DO-IN HOSHI

O'er th' world doth evil aye hold sway
I deemed, and far I fled away
    Amid the hills:
    But there the deer's sad cry, too,
thrills.
        KWO-TAI-KO-GU NO TAIU

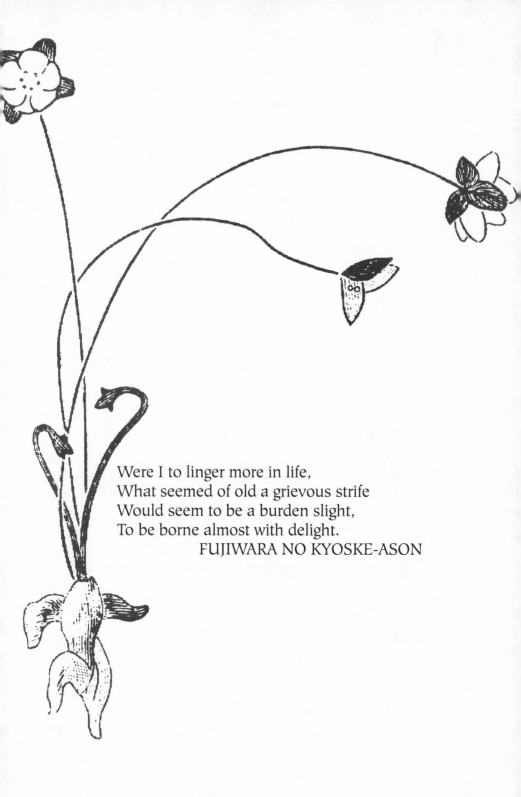

Were I to linger more in life,
What seemed of old a grievous strife
Would seem to be a burden slight,
To be borne almost with delight.
FUJIWARA NO KYOSKE-ASON

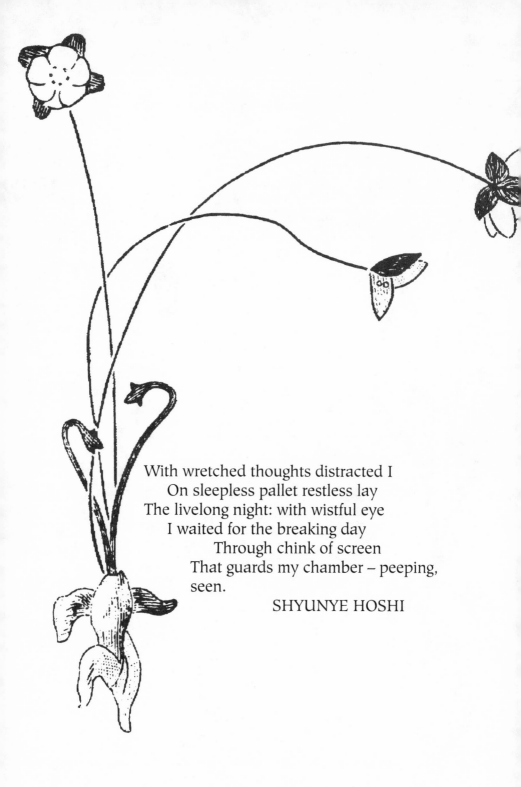

With wretched thoughts distracted I
On sleepless pallet restless lay
The livelong night: with wistful eye
I waited for the breaking day
    Through chink of screen
  That guards my chamber – peeping,
seen.

        SHYUNYE HOSHI

With deeper melancholy sways
   The moonlit night my love-sick soul;
See how my face my woe betrays,
   How down my cheek the tears roll.
           SAI-GO HOSHI

The passing shower onwards sweeps, –
Not yet upon the yew-leaves dried
Its scattered drops, – and lo! there creeps
The rising mist up yon hill-side
    Of autumn e'en,
    At twilight's chilly hour seen.
                    J'YAKUREN HOSHI

I would that I might show to thee
    The island-fisher's oft-drenched sleeve,
I would that thine own eyes might see
    How the salt waves their tints ne'er
    thieve;
        From mine, alas!
Aye tear-bedewed, the colors pass.
      IN-FU-MON IN NO TAIU

Now grasshopper's chirp the livelong night
I hear, now hoar-frost doth the ground
O'ercarpet, and in saddened plight,
My day-worn raiment yet unbound,
I strive in vain
On lonely couch repose to gain.
DAIJO-DAIJIN

My sleeve is as the rock unseen,
　　Ne'er bared at lowest ebb of tide,
　And none do guess my grief, I ween,
Now how my tear-drenched sleeve's ne'er
　　dried.

NIJO NO IN SAMAKI

O that throughout an endless life
I might in peace dwell, far from strife!
For ever watch the fishing yawl,
And view the nets abundant haul:
How fair to me,
How pleasant such a lot would be!
KAMAKURA NO UDAIJIN

Now autumn-gusts sweep
Down Miyoshino's steep,
   And far into the night so drear
The sound of beating of the cloth,
Borne to me on the night-wind forth,
   From my lonely village home, I hear.
SANGI MASATSUNE

An ignorant man am I, unfit
  O'er all the multitude of men
In dignity supreme to sit:
  The simple priest's black robe again
    I would, a humble dweller on
    Wagatasoma, gladly don.
      SAKI NO DAI-SO-JO JI-YEN

Some men me love, some men me hate
  Inspire: whene'er I think upon
This miserable world, my fate
  More pitiable doth seem to me.
          GOTOBA NO IN

9   780785 813729